MASTERcrit.

ORO Editions
Publishers of Architecture, Art, and Design

Gordon Goff: Publisher

www.oroeditions.com
info@oroeditions.com

Published by ORO Editions

Book Design by Nick Zukauskas and Jake Anderson
Edited by Jasmine Benyamin
Managing Editor: Jake Anderson

10 9 8 7 6 5 4 3 2 1 First Edition

ISBN: 978-1-940743-94-3

Color Separations and Printing: ORO Group Ltd.
Printed in China.

ORO Editions makes a continuous effort to minimize the overall carbon footprint of its publications. As part of this goal, ORO Editions, in association with Global ReLeaf, arranges to plant trees to replace those used in the manufacturing of the paper produced for its books. Global ReLeaf is an international campaign run by American Forests, one of the world's oldest nonprofit conservation organizations. Global ReLeaf is American Forests' education and action program that helps individuals, organizations, agencies, and corporations improve the local and global environment by planting and caring for trees.

MASTERcrit.

ORO
EDITIONS
Novato, CA

2015
2016
2017

contents.

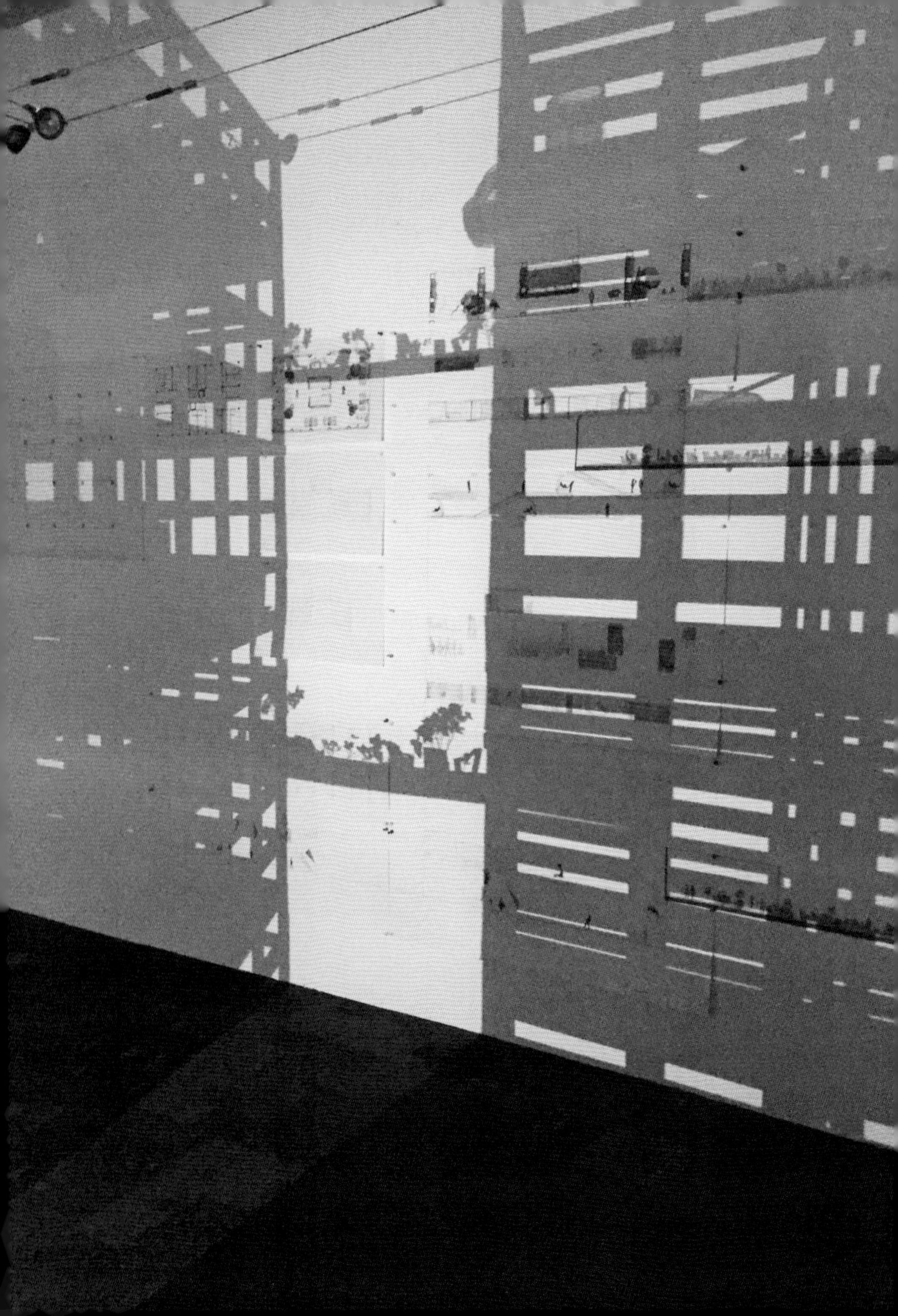

foreword.

Opposite: Photo by Sarah Traver

There are over 150 schools of architecture in the United States, and we all strive to give the best education to our students that we can, exposing them to new, engaging ideas and challenging them to open their minds to new possibilities in the exploration of physical space.

Much of this engagement is derived from the excellence of our faculty, but where possible, novel perspectives in concentrated bursts from visiting luminaries add a powerful impetus to stimulating the student learning experience.

While cost and distance can be impediments to bringing the best minds in the world to campus, UWM is fortunate to benefit from the vision of its supporters, specifically the David and Julia Uihlein Charitable Foundation, to underwrite such programs as MASTERcrit. Launched in 2015 under the able direction of Dr. Jasmine Benyamin, the workshop series gives a highly selective group of students exposure and access to some of the leading figures in contemporary architecture in a focused, intensive charrette.

The results of the first three MASTERcrits are brought together in this volume, demonstrating the power of the charrette and the potency of exploring novel methods and viewpoints within a conventional curriculum. We are grateful to the faculty, staff, donors, and students, but most of all to the MASTERcritics for lending their time, energy, and expertise toward the pedagogical enrichment of our school.

—Bob Greenstreet
Dean, School of Architecture and Urban Planning, University of Wisconsin-Milwaukee

Master class ***[/ˈmɑ:stəˌklɑ:s/]***

-noun

1. A class or session given to exceptional students of a particular discipline by an expert of the discipline—usually music, but also painting, drama, or any of the arts—on an occasion where skills are being developed.

MASTERcrit ***[/ˈmɑ:stəˌcrit/]***

-noun

1. A week-long charrette undertaken by the best graduating students in the School of Architecture, bracketed by lectures and presentations undertaken by MASTERcritics. 2. A publication documenting the results of the workshop, alongside essays by the MASTERcritics and related works.

Below: Annual "Charette Club" race through the streets of Paris, 1927.

introduction.

Modeled on the traditional notion of a "Master Class," MASTERcrit was conceived in 2015 as a hybrid series of events that encompassed lectures, critiques, and a charrette that enlisted the best graduating students of architecture at the University of Wisconsin-Milwaukee School of Architecture and Urban Planning (SARUP). Each year, a guest MASTERcritic was invited to present a project brief to the team that in some way reflected a current pre-occupation in their practice and research. Students in turn were asked to produce artifacts in an immersive setting that manifested their responses.

Ultimately, they engaged a set of questions within and outside the project proposals; while the work was evaluated via the relatively conventional confines of a "crit," a primary goal of the enterprise as a whole was to ask how and in what ways could design—as discipline and practice—mediate pedagogy and the profession?

I could not think of better guests to inaugurate the MASTERcrit program than the New York-based practice MOS Architects, comprised of Hilary Sample and Michael Meredith. They write, they draw, they build, they talk, they make films—in short, they tell stories that effortlessly straddle big and small questions.

The problem they asked the students to consider was located in the Menil neighborhood of Houston. This site is familiar to MOS—a place where art and life mingle freely. Students were challenged to re-think two dwelling types—the bungalow and the garage-apartment—for the 21st century. How could these house types be conceived of as at once relaxed and rigorous, as places where the ordinary and everyday gesture toward the sublime?

"Some cities are nice." Thus began a series of conversations between the students and the MASTERcritic for 2016, Los Angeles-based architect and pedagogue Andrew Zago. When asked to describe his practice, he referred to it in part as "post-ironic." Meant as a counterpoint to the "object ontology" that had mesmerized his younger colleagues, his interest was in part to develop "tactics aimed at undermining the object-nature of things."

Operating under the moniker "Big Dumb Building," he presented the team with the following prompt: can cities (and Chicago in particular) be defined as agglomerations of "shaped things" made up of buildings behaving not unlike unruly guests at a party? The resultant work (and not unlike Zago's own projects and writing) indexed a mash up of popular culture, intermingled with past and present zeitgeists. What he coined "awkward displays of expertise" were encircled by form making that channeled Godzilla, via full frontal facadism, slapstick tectonics, and "too big to fail" scale.

In its third iteration, MASTERcrit 2017 was led by Berlin -based architect Jürgen Mayer H. As in 2016, Mayer set his eyes on the city of Chicago. Entitled "TOGETHER.WHENEVER," the proposal suggested using Mies van der Rohe's 860/880 Lakeshore Drive Apartments as a staging ground to examine new live/work scenarios ushered by the sharing economy. Students engaged this charged site as an operative historic precedent. In part an homage to Sol Lewitt's *Incomplete Cubes*, they maintained the structural frames of the buildings but infused them with alternative programmatic proposals better suited to the demands of contemporary society.

Mayer deployed the concept of "shared-separation" (coined by art historian and theorist John Paul Ricco), as a design tool of sorts, in order to imagine new narratives of cooperative dwelling. Could these icons be regarded as a palimpsest—buildings whose history could be subverted and remade, or again in Ricco's words, "unbecome"? Mayer's most valuable lesson lay in the way in which he challenged our shared historical ties to the canon of Bauhaus modernism. By championing progressive programming, he urged students to embrace the existing physical environment, to graft new futures onto old pasts.

I often refer to architecture as the historian Robin Evans did, within the framework of translation between ideas and objects. The MASTERcrit model invited outside practitioners to share their pedagogical expertise, encourage experimentation, and foster productive speculation. They asked the students to re-think the discursive gaps between thinking and making, and in so doing unmasked particular institutional biases.

MOS, Andrew Zago, and Jürgen Mayer H. each in their own way is invested in means and methods that instantiate lateral thinking—not just across disciplines, but also discourses, politics, geographies, economies, and scales. They see it as their task not to re-invent architecture, but to think through it.

—Jasmine Benyamin, PhD
Associate Professor at the School of Architecture and Urban Planning, University of Wisconsin-Milwaukee

2015

house.
housing.
+
art.

"I came up with a concept...we would rotate the works of art... The public would never know museum fatigue. Works would appear, disappear, and reappear like actors on a stage. Each time they would be seen with a fresh eye."

—Dominique de Menil

Below: D. Jules Gianakos via *ArchDaily*

MOS Architects.

project brief.

For this charrette, students are asked to focus on the subject of housing. Their brief is to design a prototypical house that rethinks the type in relation to performance art. Students will begin by examining two house types located within the Menil neighborhood of Houston, Texas, which was founded by philanthropists and patrons Dominique and John Menil. This setting is unique because it is where art and life comingle and are mediated through the various structures. Art (with all its various implications) is housed within a series of iconic buildings, the Menil Collection Gallery (Renzo Piano, 1986), the Mark Rothko Chapel (Philip Johnson, 1971), the Cy Twombly Gallery (Renzo 1995), and the Menil Institute for Drawing and Study Center (Johnston Marklee, 2016). Piano viewed art in a more personal way and conceived of continually rotating exhibitions from Rothko to Newman, from Johns to Warhol.

The Foundation is currently reworking their campus. In 2009, David Chipperfield was commissioned to create a new master-plan, which preserved the adjacent bungalows, characterizing them as "hidden" and "precious." In 2014, a new restaurant was erected that mimicked the form of a bungalow in order to blend into the site. As part of this project the entry gateway was built to include a Michael van Valkenburgh landscape and parking area, further formalizing this distinctive neighborhood. In relation to the signature buildings that house significant artworks, everyday domesticity is situated within two commonplace house types: the gabled roof garage-apartment and the bungalow

a garage-apartment: A stand alone structure where the apartment is built on top of the garage's walls, and has a separate entrance typically located at the top of an exterior stair.

a bungalow: A stand alone structure, is a house with a gabled roof, covered porches, and without a basement.

While both suburban types can be found in major cities throughout the United States, the bungalow is the dominant form here, while the garage-apartment is more novel and potentially more robust as an economic model. The series of bungalows that surround the Menil complex are set back from the street edge and have various lawns and landscapes. Not all the structures are used as dwellings. Some interiors have been converted into live-work spaces with offices for art-related use. The Menil Foundation owns all the bungalows and garage-apartments, and its offices occupy several of the structures alongside the bookstore and restaurant. The rest are rented and serve as income properties. All of the bungalows have been painted gray to match the galleries. However, according to a conservation analysis, the structures were originally painted white.

Houston is one of the fastest growing cities in the United States and offers the opportunity to rethink new forms for houses and housing. As a point of departure, students are asked to undertake preliminary research into the types and analyze any typical components as well as distinctions. We believe the act of designing enables a critical way of looking at the physical world. Here, in this unprecedented setting, we fix our eyes not only on dwelling but also on urban life as a whole.

Houston has a housing shortage and the garage-apartment can be re-envisioned to develop a new form that speaks to a particular "subset" of the city that is not completely defined. As a new model for the Menil neighborhood and the Museum District more broadly, what cultural and social dimensions can be understood through the contemporary American house? What variations on these forms can be considered? How does this modified type tackle issues relating to efficiency, density, and aesthetics? How does the garage element play a key role as either part of the domestic space or as a public extension of the street? How can these latter landscaped elements serve as informal or relaxed settings on the one hand as for formal and structured on the other?

—Hilary Sample and Michael Meredith

MOS Architects

Kick Off

March 13, 2015

Charrette

March 14–22, 2015

Pin Up

March 26, 2015

Nick ZUKAUSKAS
M.Arch 2015

Andrew CESARZ
BSAS 2015

Hugh SOWARD
BSAS 2015

Jared MATERNOSKI
BSAS 2015

Anthony MEYER
M.Arch 2016

Sarah TRAVER
BSAS 2015

Gerri WHITTHUUN
M.Arch 2016

Anna DORAN
M.Arch 2016

Kelly YUEN
M.Arch 2015

Tessa BEGAY
BSAS 2015

Efrain CANO
M.Arch 2016

Justin SAGER
BSAS 2015

charette.

student work.

research.

This matrix of images catalogs part of the Menil neighborhood divorced from its respective whole to produce a holistic genericism. Dappled light, accessorized sidewalks, ad-hoc amenities, hide-and-seek promenades, golf carts, and repossessed vegetation form emergent themes throughout the neighborhood residences.

Menil Site Evolution

These diagrams show the evolution of the Menil Foundation over the last 60+ years, and how the neighborhood has been changed to accommodate its expansion.

RIGHT: Menil neighborhood figure-ground

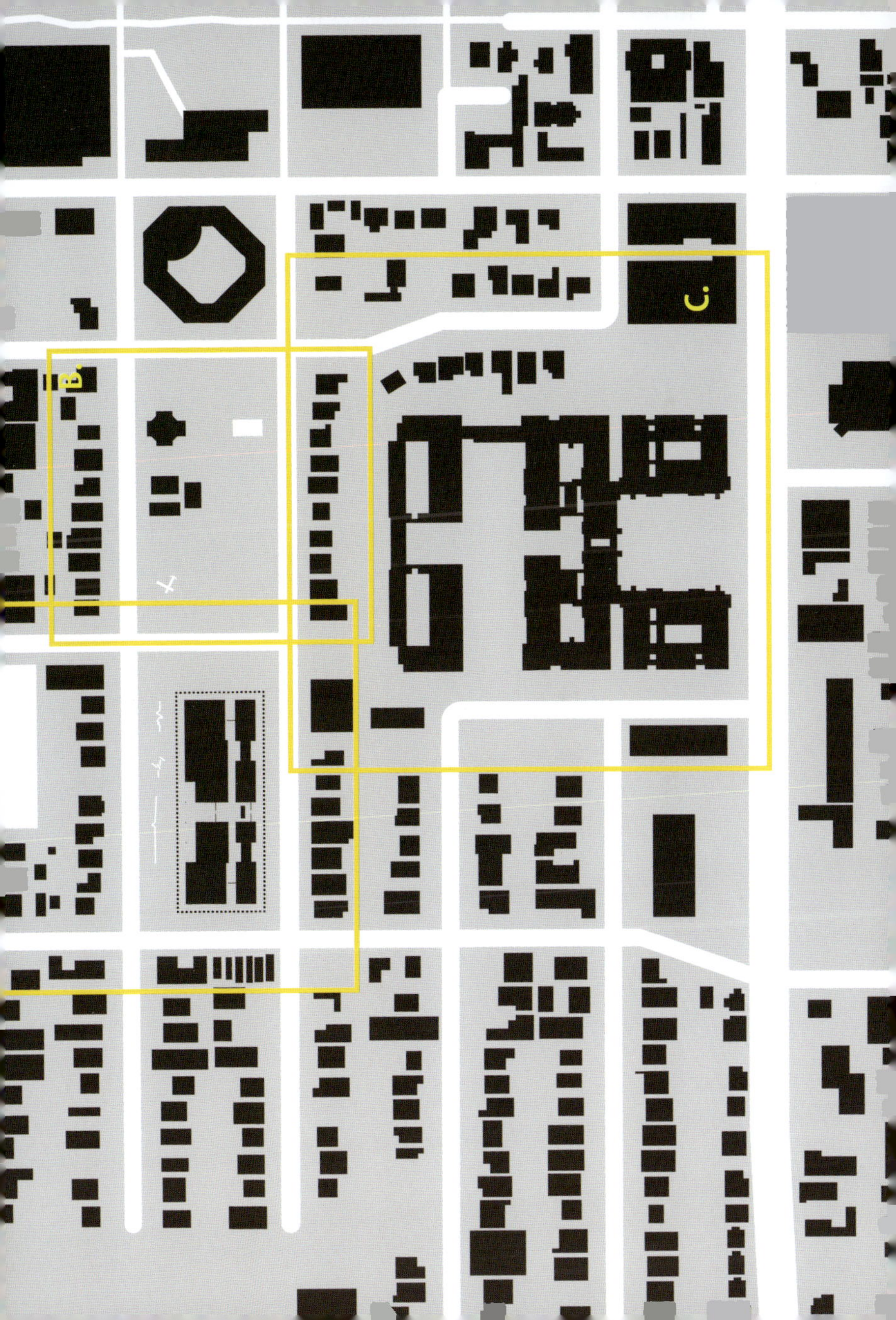
B.
C.

A

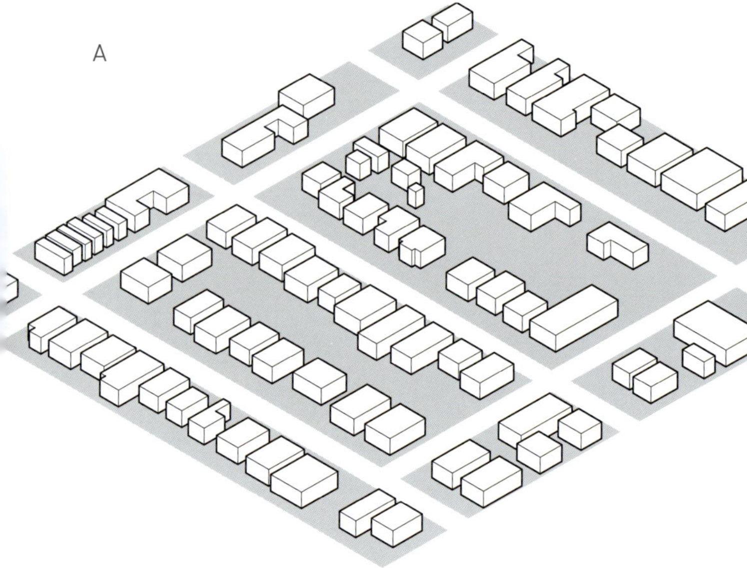

ca. 1953

Google

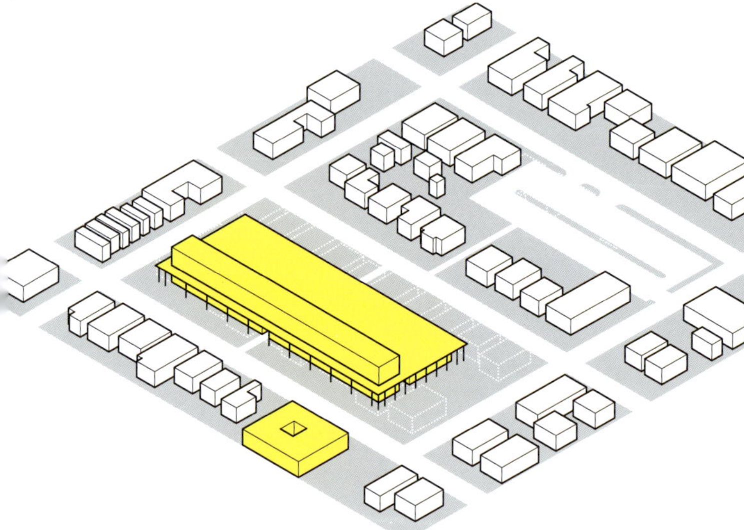

ca. 1987

+ Menil Collection
+ Cy Twombly Gallery
Google

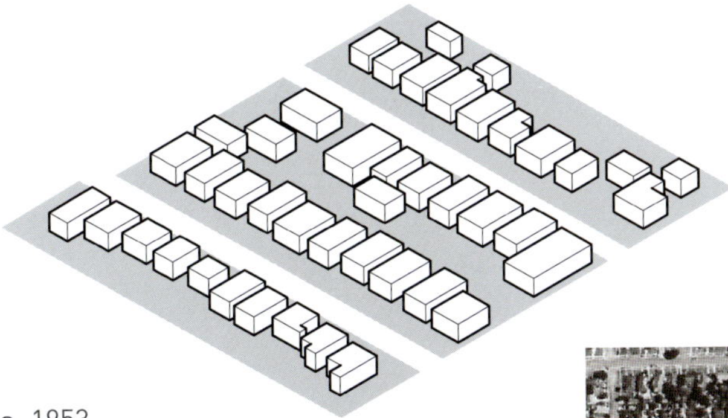

ca. 1953

Google

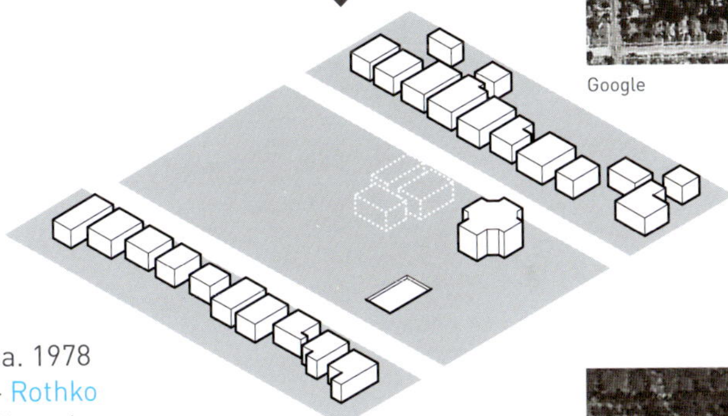

ca. 1978
+ Rothko
Chapel

Google

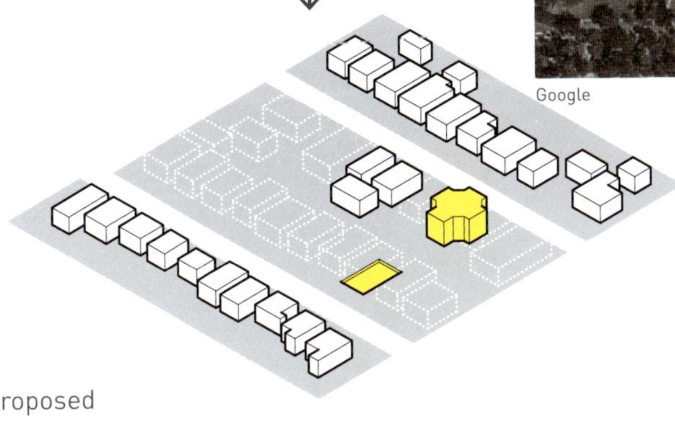

Proposed

C

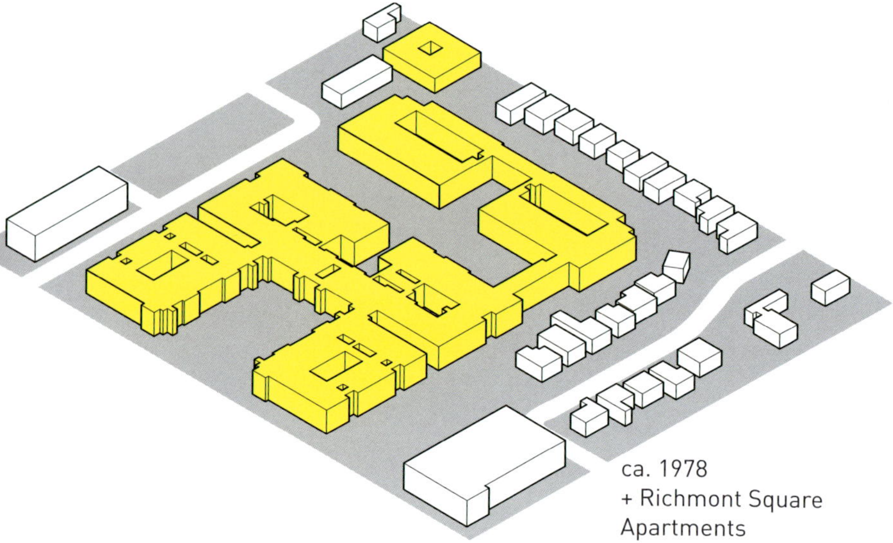

ca. 1978
+ Richmont Square Apartments
+ Cy Twombly Gallery

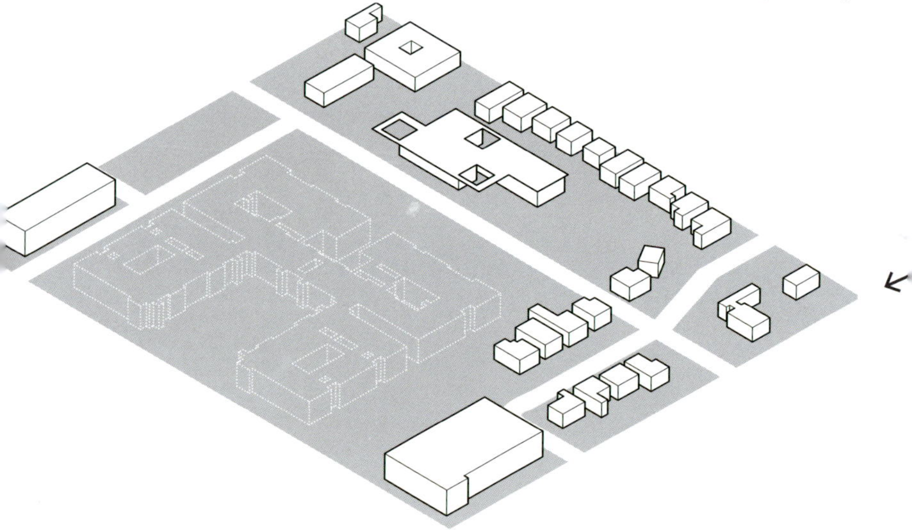

Proposed

→

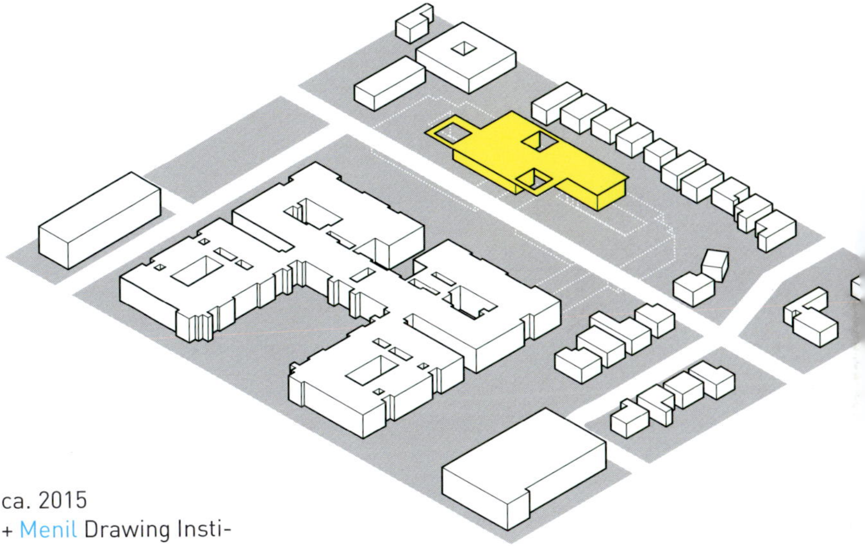

ca. 2015
+ Menil Drawing Institute

Google

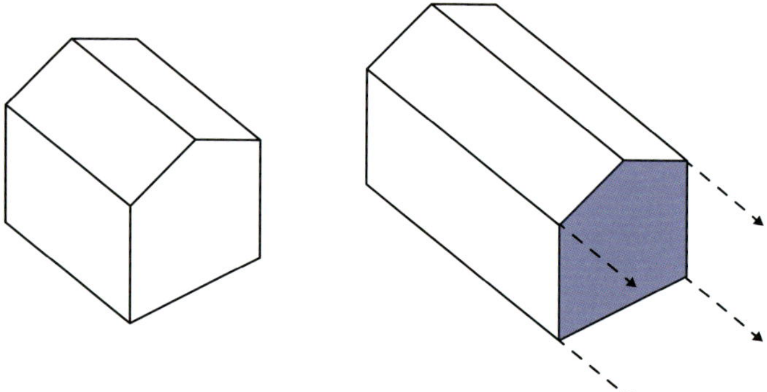

Parti Diagram

nick zukauskas.

student work.

Idealized as temporary housing for artists, this proposal confronts issues of privacy and performance, playing with visibilities, lighting, and perforation to create a dwelling that can come alive and strengthen the Menil neighborhood. A CLT cladding system presents a kind of floating facade. The extrusion of the frame on one elevation creates a forecourt, while at the rear of the building, the living area is compressed at the top floor to allow for flexible programming below.

Opposite: Section Perspective

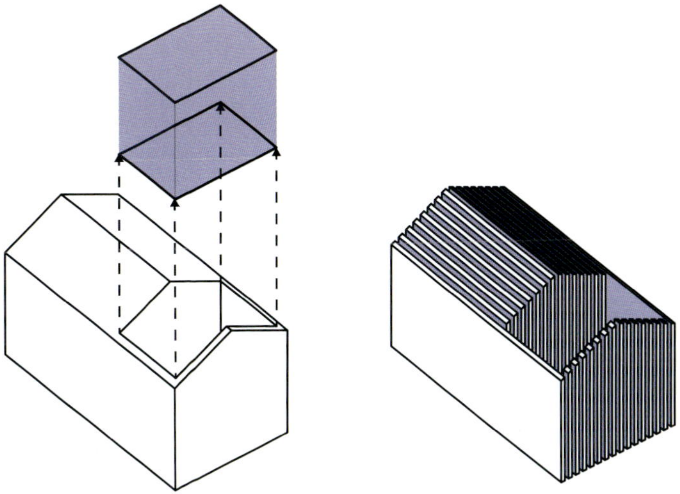

Front Elevation

Opposite bottom and left: Massing and detail models

Front Rendering

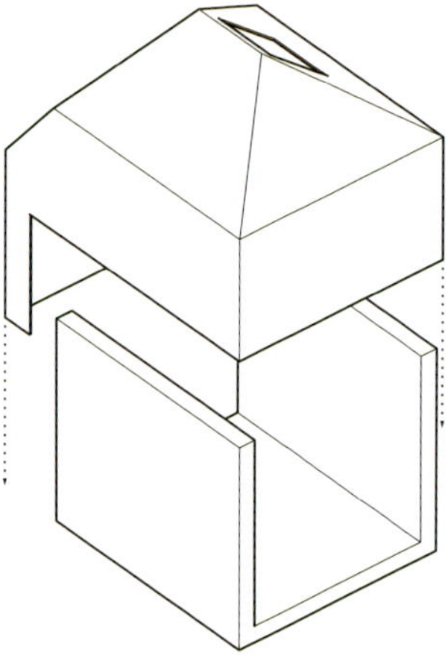

andrew cesarz.

In this proposal, the biggest design move occurs at the first floor, which is transformed into an unprogrammed, transparent box. In contrast, the living space above is more spatially articulated. Walls are thickened to accommodate carved niches. A large picture window looks onto the backyard, and circulation via a stair culminates in a sky box. One could imagine a cluster of these units creating a glowing landscape at the ground level.

Opposite bottom and below: Parti Diagrams

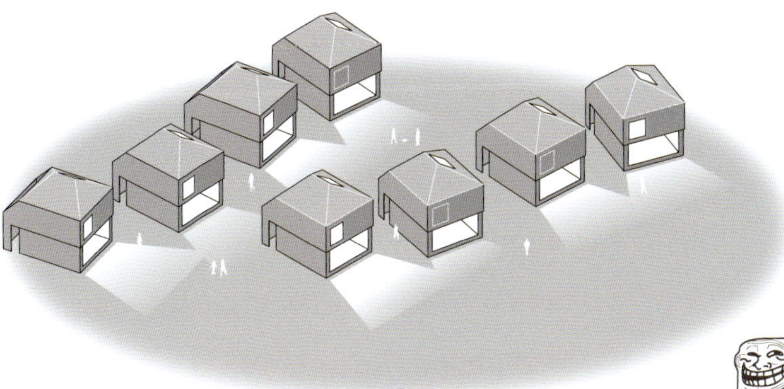

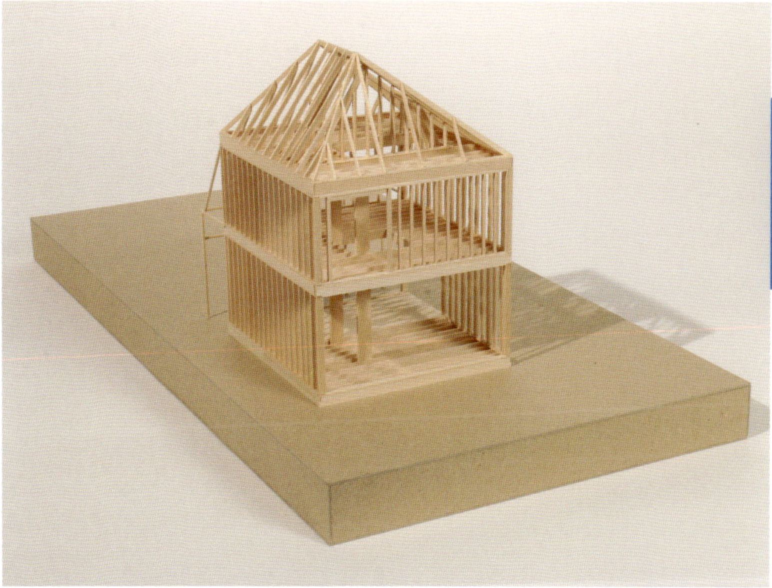

Parti Diagrams

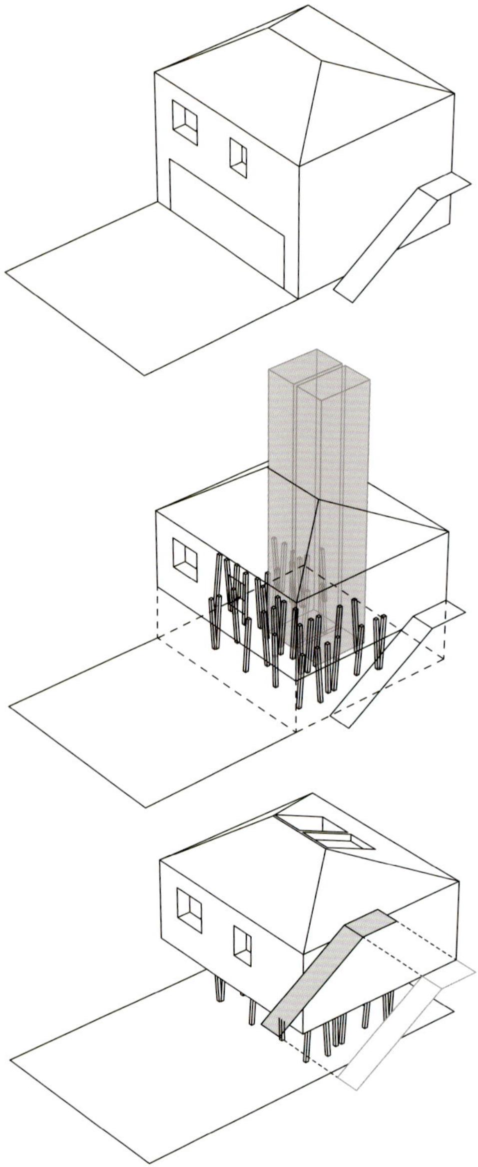

hugh soward.

The garage-apartment is a generic formal type that houses a generic program. This proposal begins in an unconventional place: the bathroom. Occupying a central position in plan and propped up in section on a plinth, this "think tank" is lit from above and below. Since the entire ground floor is also lifted by a forest of columns, the formally enclosed garage is dissolved, and a stair is needed to enter the bifurcated living space.

Section Perspective

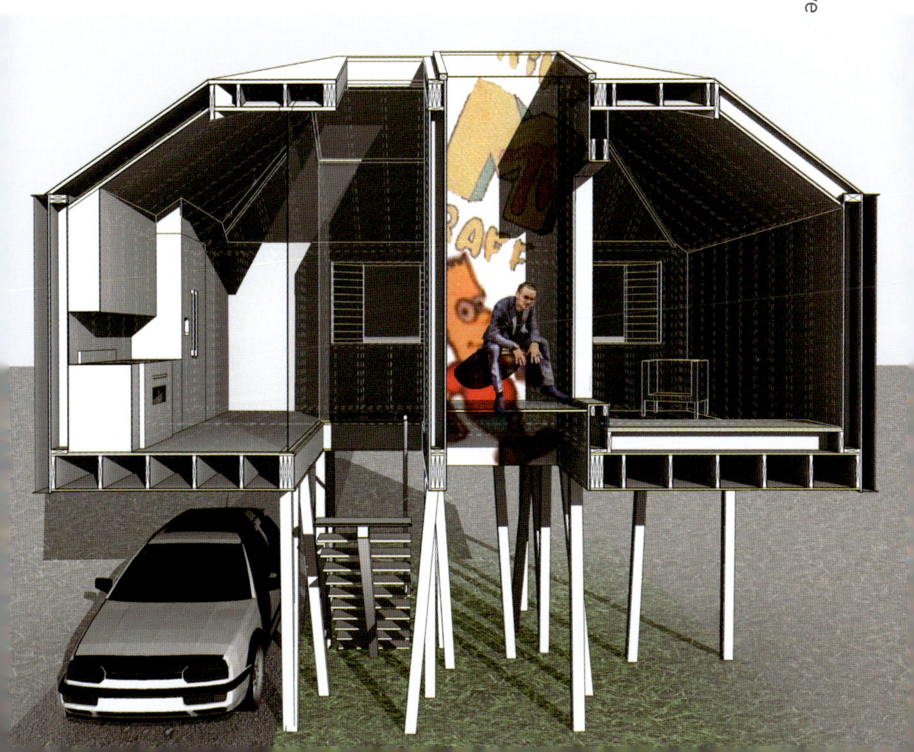

Model photos

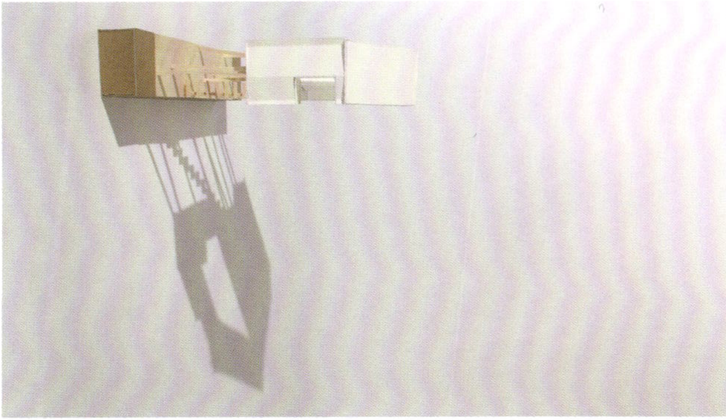

Section Perspective

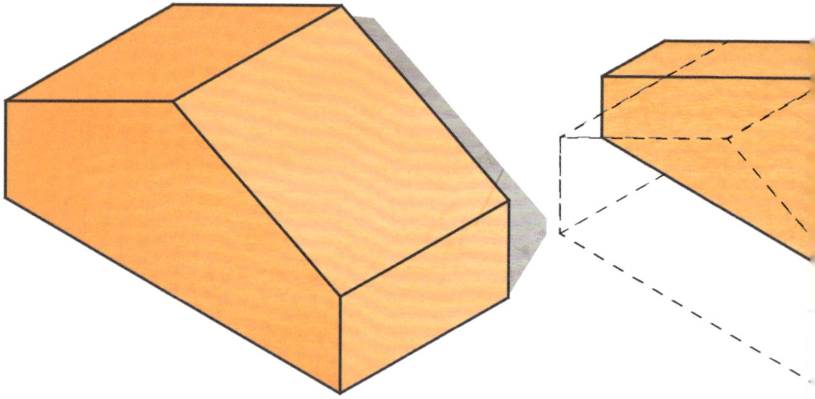

jared maternoski.

Bungalows are typically conceived as single-family dwellings. They have low-slung gable roofs and living areas that recede behind covered porches. On the other hand, the garage-apartment has a fundamentally vertically oriented composition. This proposal attempts to combine these two rather banal systems, while maintaining their essential individual features. Formally, it is narrower and longer. The interior programming is elevated to allow for a green space below.

Below: Parti Diagrams

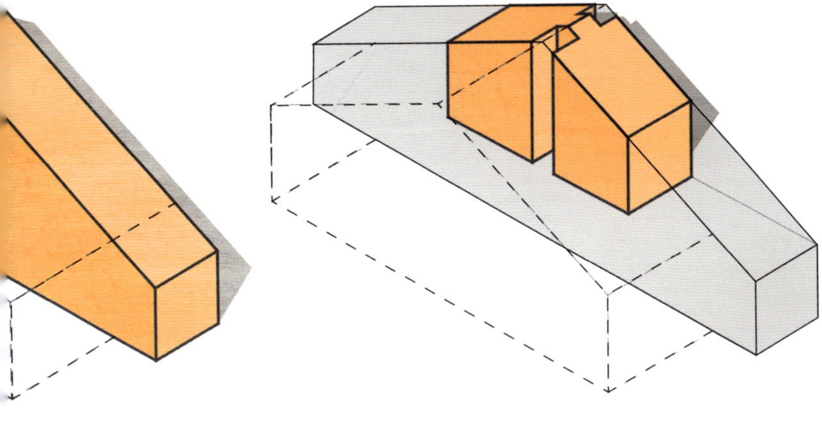

anna doran.

This proposal retains the essential sectional configuration of the garage-apartment, but its light conditions are re-imagined. The stair maintains its position on the side elevation, but now it is enclosed and cantilevered. The darkest area in the section is the garage. As you exit the space and ascend the stairs, you experience beams of light. Once upstairs, the light-filled room comprises large windows that express the faceting on the exterior elevations.

gerri witthun.

This project re-imagines the segmented nature of the garage-apartment type. Rather than adding a stair to the outside of the unit, circulation becomes a central component of the living area. There is also a stretching of the unit to extend the length the massing to the rear of the lot. Parking is buried and occupies the same footprint as the space above. The gable roof is kept in order to maintain a continuity with the rest of the street.

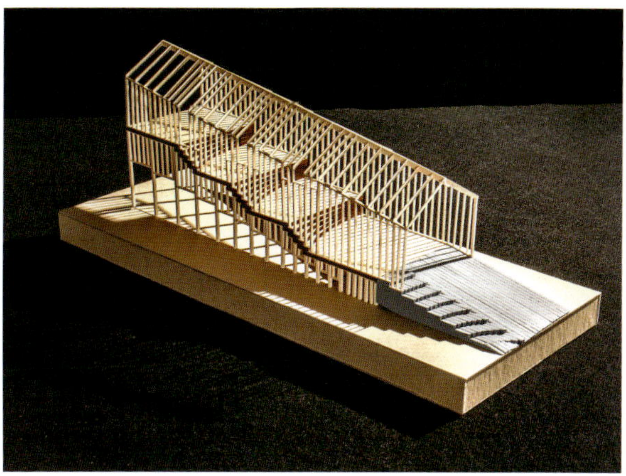

anthony meyer.

This proposal comprises three conceptual elements: genericity on the exterior, novelty in the interior, and an embedded volume. Two garage-apartments are merged back to back. On the street side, the garage is pushed back, the gabled-roof profile is lifted to create a covered porch below, and an exterior stair leads to a vaulted sleeping area. The rear retains its original massing and appears to have maintained its original configuration. The section, however, reveals an open and undulating lattice work of CLT with carved out volumes.

MOS Architects

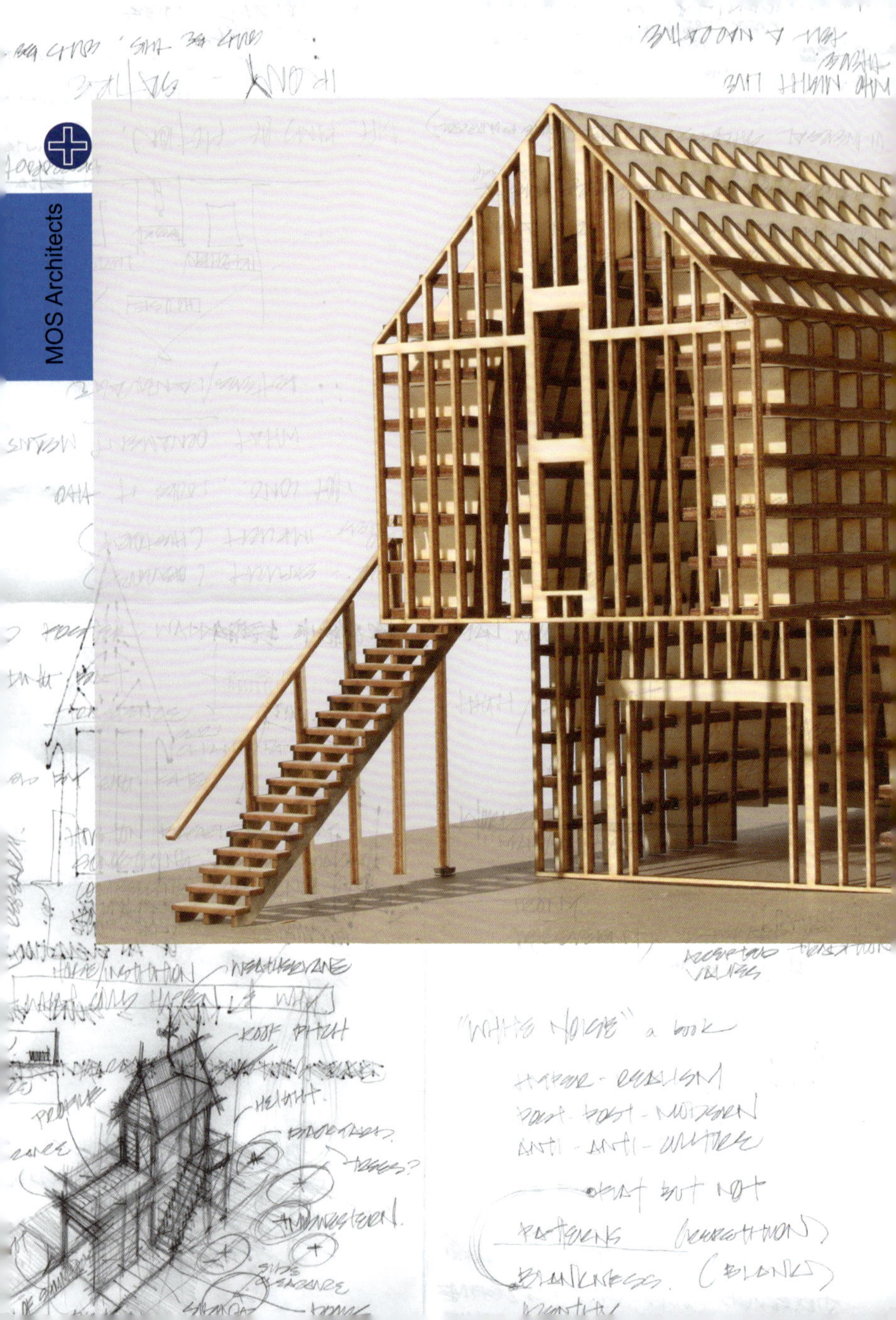

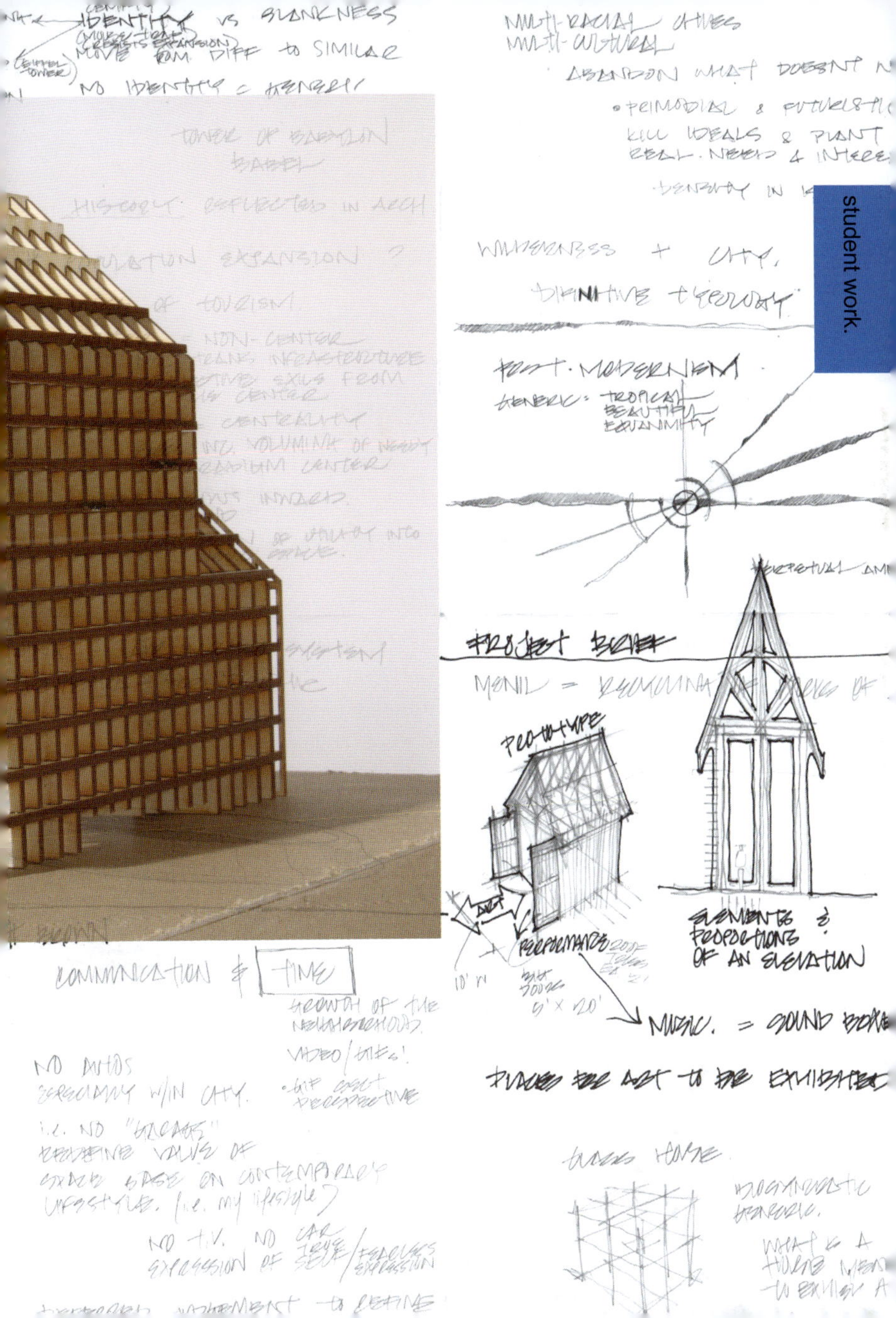

student work.

critique.

"What is the distinction between modesty and banality? And how do these words cycle back to the concept of the generic?"

—MOS

in conversation.

MOS Architects

Photo: Michael Vahrenwald

MOS Architects

Hilary Sample | Michael Meredith
with Jasmine Benyamin

in conversation.

Jasmine Benyamin
Why did you frame the studio around the subject of housing?

Hilary Sample + Michael Meredith
Housing is a rich subject for study in any architecture program. There is a long history of housing in the United States that excludes it as part of a broader design discussion. Since the 1932 MoMA International Style exhibition, housing (which incidentally had its own subsection) has been segregated from the rest of design culture. Today, housing has never been more urgently needed, and there is evidence in places such as Paris, Copenhagen, and Mexico City where design is part of a larger culture where housing is not excluded from this conversation and production. Milwaukee has a relatively recent history of housing with a few types that are found in a number of other cities across the United States and Midwest specifically. We wanted to explore how housing types and their surroundings in other contexts could be studied and compared to Milwaukee.

JB
How can Houston be a test case or model for re-thinking this housing type in other cities? Or are there particular characteristics—besides the relative lack of zoning—of Houston that provide fertile ground for these domestic scenarios?

HS
We were interested in exploring with the students the history of the neighborhood of The Menil Collection and to look at it specifically for its role as an arts campus as well as its function as a neighborhood that includes housing. What is the relationship between the houses and the institutions adjacent to them? What are those houses like? They are a specific type—mostly bungalows—which can be found in Houston but also in

Milwaukee. It is also one that is associated with the working class. At the Menil campus, they are arranged in series with park frontage. The exteriors remain original, yet some interior programming has been converted into flex and mixed use.

It's an exceptional area set within the city of Houston—a city that is confronting complex issues from growth, lack of zoning, often conflicting densities, climatic and environmental fluxes, population shifts, etc. Although now largely subsumed by the art institutions, the neighborhood nonetheless features very specific house types including bungalows, garage-apartments, and accessory dwelling units (ADU), to name a few.

They represent housing typically for workers and are made from straightforward materials. We are interested in tapping into this history. Who resides there? How are these forms constructed? What makes them not generic? The buildings need to be evaluated as a collective, but also as individual structures.

JB

One of the readings that you assigned the students was Rem Koolhaas's *Generic City*. Why this reading and how did it help the students understand Houston better?

MM

One of the conversations that occurred in the review centered on the topic of value—land and otherwise—how is value measured? The neighborhood includes priceless art but also an everyday dwelling type. How do the two co-exist? This conversation is meant to highlight the split that has happened in the US between design of housing versus design for society at large. It also reflects on the possibility for designing smaller-scale housing to ensure space for public engagement. It is not dissimilar to the thoughts expressed by Lina Bo Bardi in her critical texts on the topic. Another discussion we had regarding the Koolhaas reading was that Houston, of course, is not Paris. The former city's identity is not as well established (or "petrified" one could argue) as the latter. Nonetheless, thinking about cities like Houston in the context of this essay can prove more liberating and generate new and unexpected developments.

JB

Much of the conversation also revolved around the notion of banality. You brought up some interesting questions at the review, namely, what is the distinction between modesty and banality? What is defined as luxury today? Can you expand on your interest in these terms as formal generators?

HS

The preoccupations among some of the students around the topic of the banal actually generated responses that were not banal. And what does this mean for housing specifically? Housing at its heart has a fundamental concern with providing dwelling through typical spaces-kitchens, bedrooms, bathrooms, etc.—but in reality all of these spaces require attention and thought. When design enters into the equation, these spaces quickly become atypical. This is at odds with the way housing is designed in the United States, especially if it is housing that is funded, because it has to comply with guidelines and specific codes. It is at this point when design is taken out of the equation and housing is reduced to building and not architecture. Looking at the design of house as opposed to housing is a way to get at this concern. In this country there has been endless building of houses en masse—suburban developments and tract housing are so generic and paired down that there is no sense of individual identity. If we think of houses in Europe for instance, we see the house as one of the most important types to be considered for design. It is a type that drives a lot of experimentation.

When we think of houses in our practice, we think of the Vanna Venturi House or Frank Gehry's own house, because they are instances where architecture has intervened directly on the house type. Not coincidentally, Gehry's house in its original form is a bungalow. Gehry's insertions and deconstruction of that house in particular created a sensation. His methods and working process were a rethinking of what the American house could become. At the same time, as much as we are interested in the work of Gehry, we also love the earthquake patterning on the Winton House, as well as Shaker design. They created a community in the form of a collection of buildings, some of which included housing, which can be read together. There are rules, and a particular set of concerns that are formal, environmental, material, etc. We explore forms that are familiar and vernacular, and then rework them to make new physical experiences. The house plan is very specific, atypical, and has certain relationships to the exterior that make it atypical and not with great depth.

JB

Another reading you advised the students to consider was Venturi Scott Brown's seminal essay on the duck and the decorated shed. Are this essay and the Koolhaas piece examples of writing that you find yourself returning to in your work?

HS

Yes, among others. I am interested in reading essays about housing, mostly written by female architects. Lina Bo Bardi to Alison Smithson, Jane Drew, but also more contemporary architects who I have written about on housing in the GSAPP Transcripts. I am also drawn to Tatiana Bilbao's work on housing.

JB

What are the dog-eared books on your office shelves at the moment?

HS

We are absorbed with the books we have and we are working on. A compendium of scale figures called *An Unfinished Encyclopedia*, a children's book with Corraini Editione and the CCA called *Houses for Sale*. We read all the time, Michael is reading about attention, I have been reading poetry, as well as a lot of children's books, and female architects and history. Of course, because I teach housing at Columbia, I am always reading about houses and housing, as well as history of housing through African American culture. This latter interest comes from learning about our street in Harlem where we live and work.

JB

The brief addressed housing, but with an interesting twist: housing within the context of contemporary art. To this end, students were asked to choose an artist who would occupy their units.

MM

It was curious how and in what way the choice of artists influenced or shaped the student's understanding of the architectural object. Given more time, they could have pushed their ideas further. They were quite committed to their hypothetical inhabitants, and their choices definitely drove some of their responses. Again, given more time, it would be interesting to see the students push them into more uncomfortable positions. Ultimately, architecture is more interesting to me than art; we must contend with real world clients and intervene in complex scenarios.

JB

How much of a role does the site—or more precisely the ground—play in your design process? You have said that you don't really talk about "site," because you find it to be a loaded term.

HS

Yes, that is right. We would rather say that we concentrate on elements of the surroundings. What is the soil made up of? Who are the neighbors? What are the qualities of the surrounding vernacular buildings? Are the materials local? What can builders do and what can we do? From my perspective, one of the most interesting outcomes here was the framing models—would you agree?

JB

Yes I would. They are not often used in studio but proved particularly instructive here.

HS

The students made beautiful structural framing models. Clearly there is a culture of making at the school, over drawing or rendering. Each school has a different set of concerns. The structural models adhere to concerns we have about straightforward forms, representing vaguely familiar forms. The models are material objects in and of themselves. They also play into the history of housing: How have houses evolved in their structural and material development? In our office, we typically work only with paper, so our suggestion that the students make basswood structural diagrams was unusual, but it afforded focusing on construction guided by the forms, not the other way around.

JB

What are your thoughts on the MASTERcrit workshop?

MOS Architects

HS

It's essential for schools to continually reinvent pedagogy with their faculty and students, as a collective project. And it is crucial to do this with outside guests in a highly selective and thoughtful way like these workshops. We were most interested to do this work with you because of your research and interest in architecture and its representation, not only through your thoughts on the Werkbund but more so your research and emphasis on the relationship of architecture and photography. Photography has been an important part of our work, since it forces us to rethink how architecture can be represented. We have also built two photography studios, so we are deeply interested in the issue of building these spaces.

MM

As I have discussed in other settings, we see our practice as "postmedium." Architecture is inherently representational. Practicing architecture—as opposed to making buildings—is highly mediated and discursive. One way to understand architectural production is that it defines a relationship between intention and representation. The goal of the discipline is to produce ideas of cultural progress through representation.

20
16

a big dumb building.

"Among the conjectures foregrounded in the show are new building postures, co-dependent structures, non-local contextualism, and perhaps most important of all, an assertion of a desire to see comedy achieve an equivalent status to tragedy in architecture, as it has for centuries in all of the other arts to the profound increase in their powers and the resultant existential benefit to each and all of us."

—Jeff Kipnis on "Figure Ground Game"

Jeff Kipnis and Stephen Turk: Figure Ground Game (2014).

ZAGO ARCHITECTURE

Contemporary cities are complex organisms. They defy easy analysis or singular characterization. Over the past one hundred years, cities have grown to such a degree that they dwarf the scale of historic human settlements. Their scales stretch the limits of comprehension. Nonetheless, cities remain a physical fact. Flows of capital, information, and resources are embedded in them. They are also composed of brute inert masses (buildings), streets, and infrastructure. These "shaped" things are unavoidable presences; to quote Winston Churchill, after they are shaped, "they shape us." Given the breadth of pressing urban concerns, architecture may sometimes seem of little importance. This workshop challenges this view by stating unequivocally: our cities urgently need new architecture, because it is architecture that provides us with unique ways of defining new forms of living.

Since the latter half of the twentieth century, the very big building in a city (VBBC) has been variously theorized, vilified, ignored, grudgingly accepted, and embraced. We now recognize them has inevitable, if occasional, products of advanced technologies, programmatic agglomerations, and flows of capital. The MASTERcrit brief posits that that are as yet unrealized diagrams for the VBBC, ones in which such buildings can become unruly guests at the city's party.

Aldo Rossi's Locomotiva 2 project for Turin (1962) is a VBBC as mute urban symbol. The building hovers implacably above a network of dynamic transportation systems. The almost exact counterpoint to this can be found four years later in Ron Herron's Walking City (1966). In this case, the building itself becomes a mode of transportation, while its form resembles an amorphic techno-bubble.

Ishiro Honda, *Godzilla* (1954)

"Urban studies never attribute significant importance to research dealing with singular urban artifacts."

—Aldo Rossi, *The Architecture of the City*

Ishiro Honda, *Godzilla* (1954)

In the ensuing decades, the VBBC matures as a type. Perhaps thinking of his own project for Euralille, Rem Koolhaas theorizes it as an end-of-architecture nothing building in an essay entitled "Bigness" (1995). In the following year, he conceives of his very own every-thing-building, the so-called Hyperbuilding in Bangkok. The project demonstrates the efficacy of unexpected urban arrangements in elevation, most strikingly employed by Peter Eisenman, Charles Gwathmey, Steven Holl, and Richard Meier's World Trade Center proposal of 2002.

In his exhibition entitled "Figure Ground Game" (2014), Jeffrey Kipnis proposed a suite of buildings intended in part as a calculated departure from the tacit expectation of good posture in buildings. Derived from my own firm's Shenzhen MOCAPE project of 2007, the buildings become overtly anthropomorphic and slouchy. Reference is made in the accompanying text to the notion of "non-local contextualism," a phrase attributed to buildings that rely only on each other for proximate context.

This workshop proposes that such belligerent tectonic behavior can have novel consequences when foisted onto an urban fabric. What begins as harmless jostling when the buildings are considered in isolation becomes boorish and potentially destructive behavior when embedded in the city. This is not just the bigness theorized in *S, M, L, XL* (1995), but rather big as an explicit affront to decorum and safety. Our model for this will be Godzilla.

While Chicago can claim credit for significantly contributing to our understanding of the VBBC, it has never (the dreary *Transformers: Dark of the Moon* from 2011 notwithstanding) been properly visited by a giant monster. In this charrette, we intend to redress this slight by reimagining the Sears Tower, again. This time as housing.

—Andrew Zago

ZAGO ARCHITECTURE

charette.

Photos: Nick Zukauskas

Dan CAUSIER
M.Arch 2016

Kim WORKMAN
BSAS 2016

Jessica LINDNER
M.Arch 2016

Jennifer BURNS
M.Arch 2016

Rachel MOMENEE
M.Arch 2016

Cody SCHUELLER
BSAS 2016

Taylor KROSLIN
BSAS 2016

Bob Allsop
M.Arch 2016

student work.

Axonometric

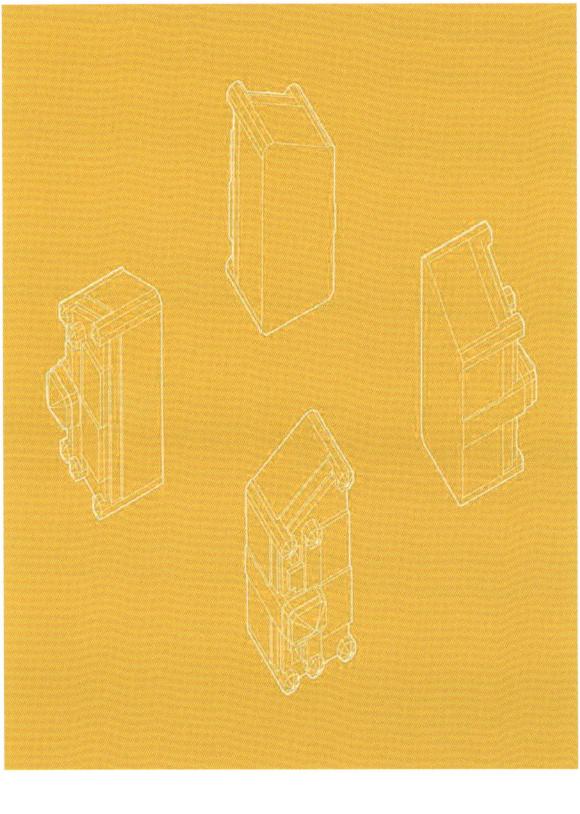

cody schueller.

student work.

The posture precedent derives from an image of Godzilla in the original 1954 *Gojira* as he makes his way to land—but not there yet—soon to make his presence known. My architecture precedent is the massively unyielding Chicago Merchandise Mart. To achieve a post-ironic authenticity, we purposely restricted our technique to two basic commands-splitting and rotating.

By deliberately reducing our maneuvers to rudimentary instructions, our new architectures appear baffling. Rather than use all the tools we know, and allowing ourselves to commit basic architectural errors, we are able to conceal our mastery. This "big dumb building" neither looks to align with or critique our relation to the original; we imagine the norm in an alternative way.

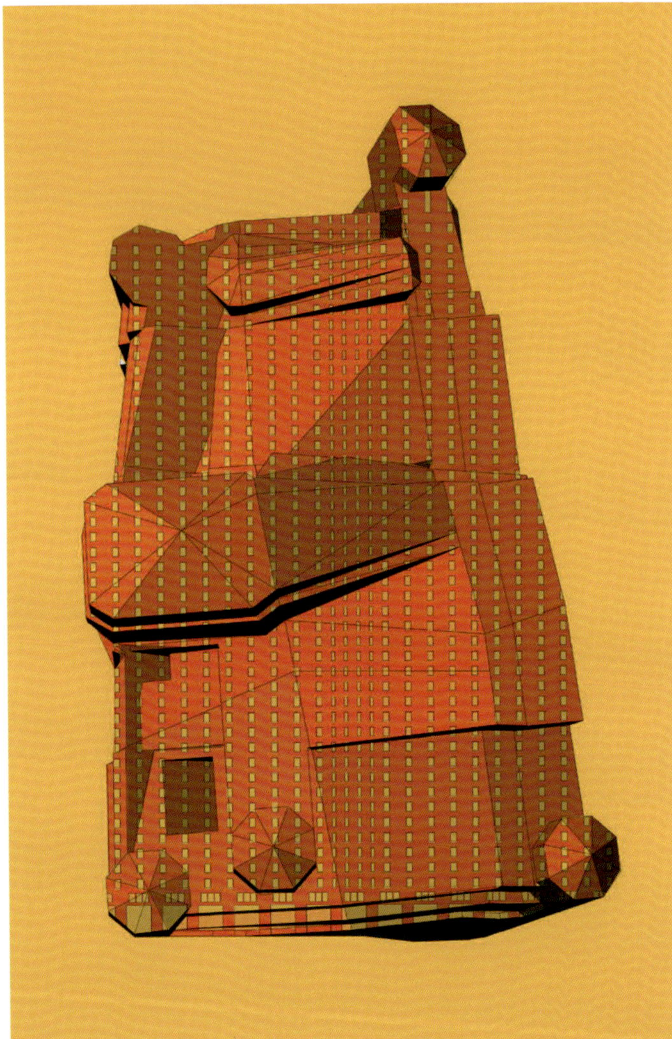

Elevation

Section

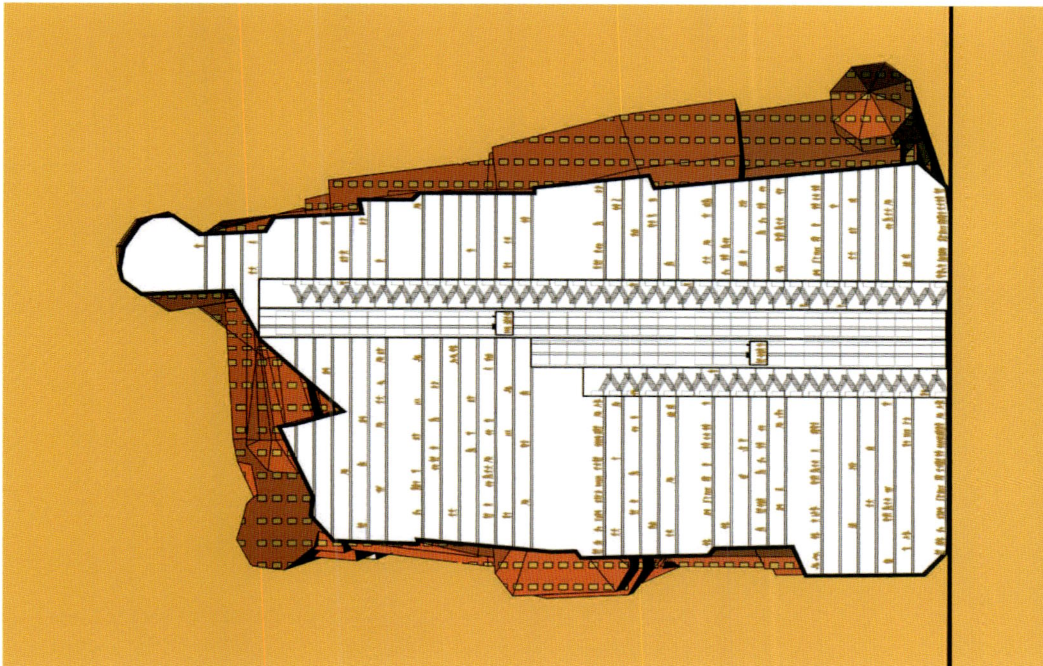

ゴジラ
がシカゴに侵入
Big, Dumb, Building

Section

rachel momenee.

Axonometric

Transported from Turin, Matte Trucco's Fiat Factory has transformed from an industrial groundscraper to a residential highrise in the heart of Chicago. Inspired by the heights of the Willis Tower, the structure's mutation consists of a series of awkward Godzilla-like movements to create a new form and figure.

bob allsop.

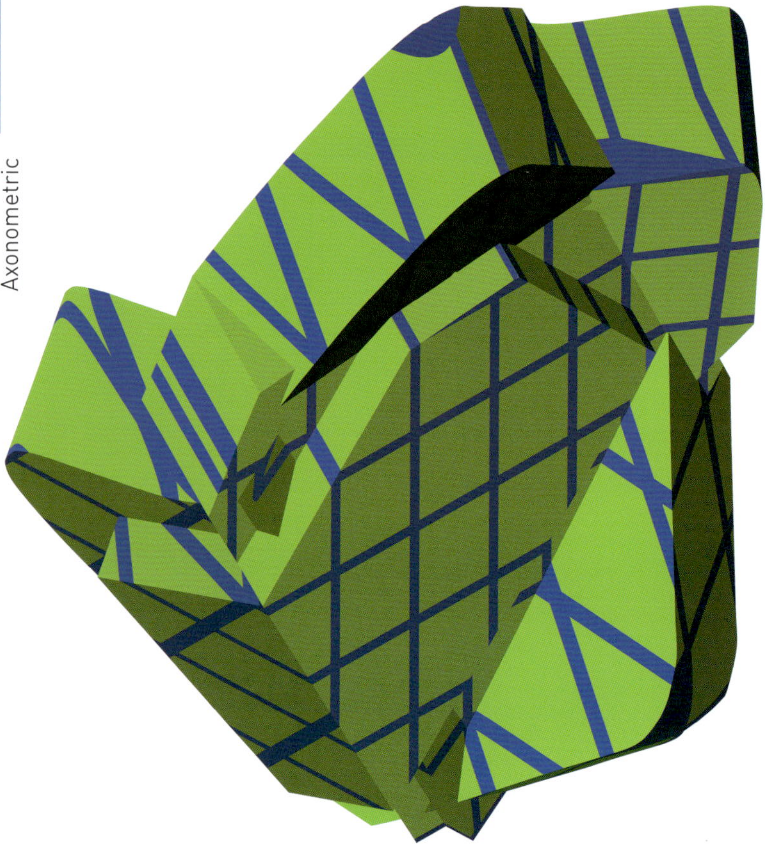

Axonometric

Section

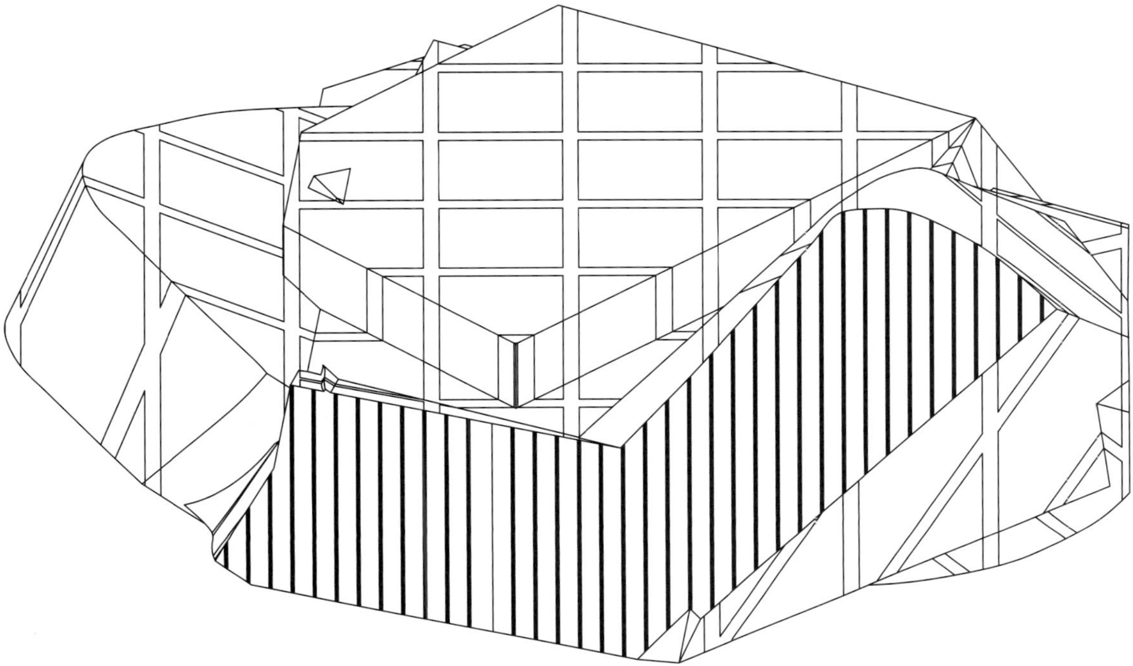

dan causier.

Godzilla may be big, but he's not flexible. When he's throwing his weight around, he does so with a limited range of motion—he's got short arms, thunder thighs, a neck that bends in the wrong places. He musters the widest stance possible and throws an elbow, but confined to the limits of his thick skin, his posture is awkward, his movements jerky. If it weren't for his breath of plasma rays (or whatever), this guy would never win a fight.

The actor inside the suit is, of course, the source of Godzilla's problems. Straining against the weight of the bulky rubber, the human scale of each movement the actor makes is blurred by the transposition of human proportions to giant lizard ones. The Tokyo-destroyer's arms, even with a big chest and armpits that truncate them closer to the elbow than a man's, most closely relate the scale of the costume to the actor's proportions; whereas the creature's gigantic legs and stomach most effectively conceal the living mechanism beneath, containing the entire hips and waist of the puppeteer within the definition of the monster's protruding belly.

Godzilla roars, sometimes celebrates, and has even been known to flop. I chose a moment in which he charges: head down, legs in a squat. Godzilla here approaches a more uncannily human position than I'd seen before, one in which the human gesture is more visible, and the nature of the obscuring physical fact of the costume—the limits to recognizing the human—is more expressed. In this pose, we can feel the strain of the performer and the difficulty of making Godzilla move in ways that read effectively despite the limitations of the characterization. In acting parlance, Godzilla demands bigness.

Pouillon's Climat de France was the unfortunate subject of contortions intended to approximate this pose. It's a building

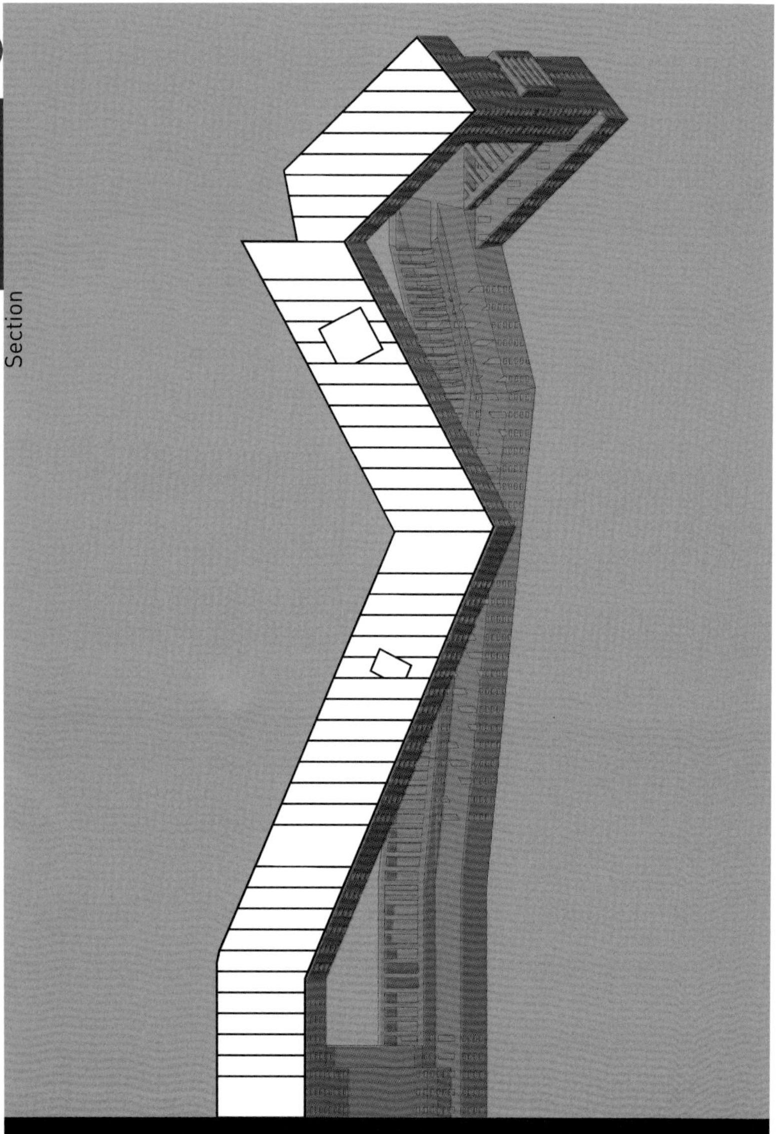

Section

that lends itself to expressing this extreme stress due to its limitations. As a loop, it is allowed to fold in upon itself, but every fold must be expressed twice. Each exacting twist results in some kind of fracture elsewhere. The many kinks of the final form, like a bone broken twice, are more pronounced in their reciprocity (and the humiliation, for this stately formal edifice, is more acute).

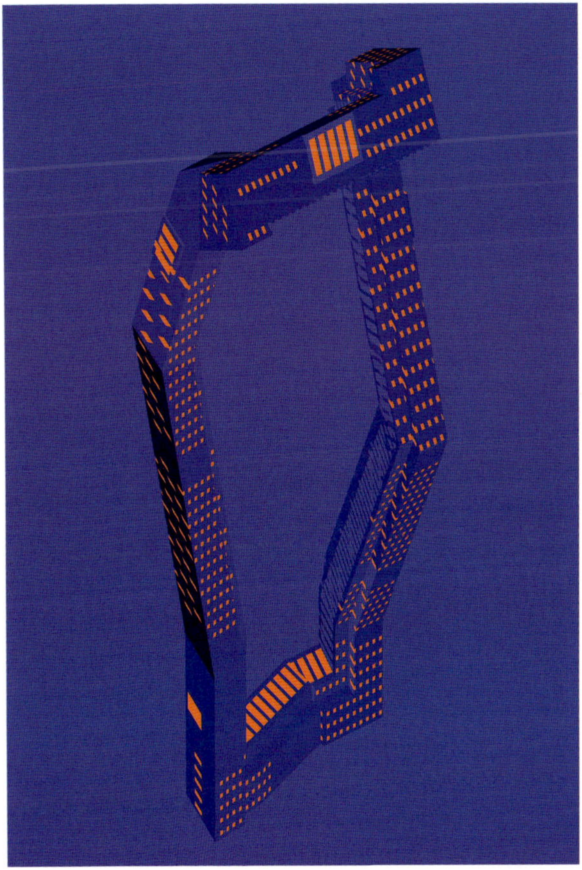

Axonometric

Section

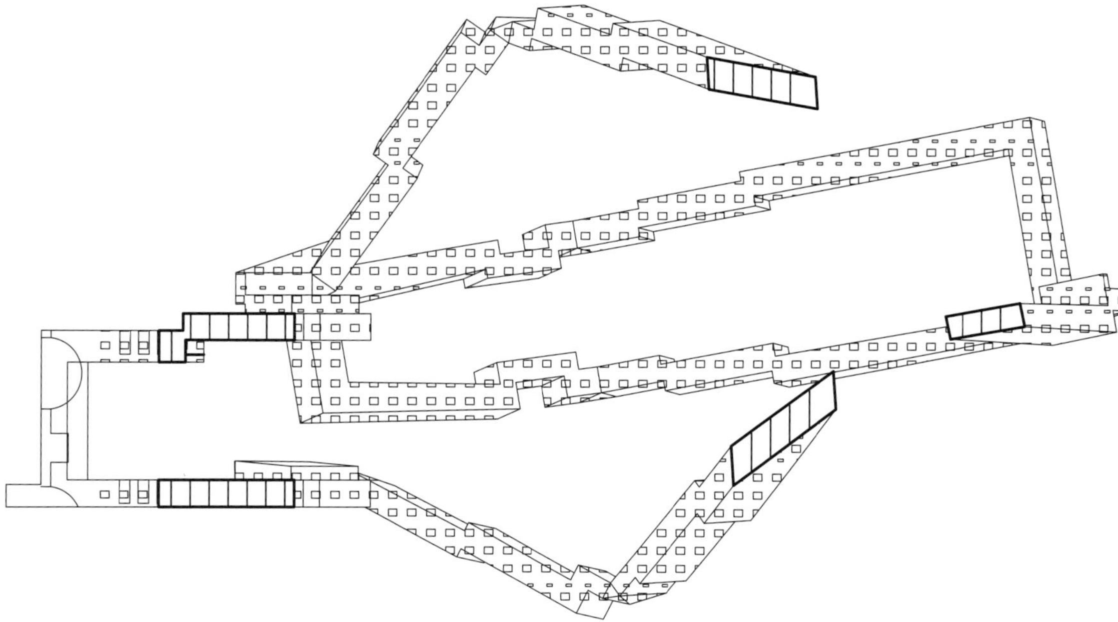

jessica lindner.

In this proposal, Godzilla's posture is cross referenced with the Karl Marx Hof in Vienna. Godzilla is not generally thought of as elegant—he stumbles around the city as he destroys it. He seems to be most awkward when he is at rest. This resting posture is superimposed by the historical precedent, now folded in half and draped over the behemoth. Each break in the cracked open surface indexes Godzilla's movements. The joints are welded in such a way to infill the resultant gaps.

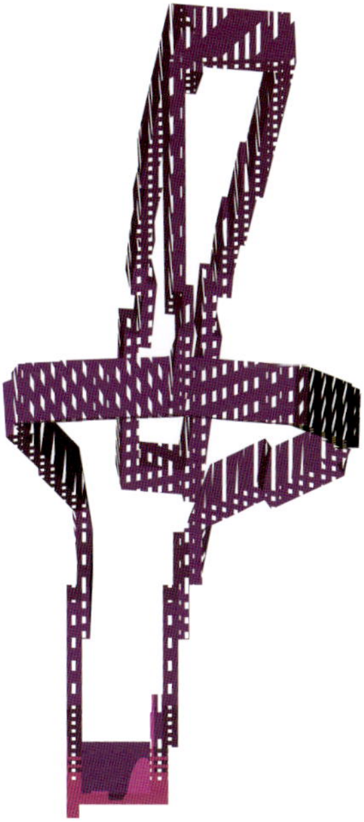

Axonometric

Round-table discussion with Andrew Zago
Guests: Antonio Furgiuele, Karl Wallick, Mo Zell, Whitney Moon, Chris Cornelius
Photo: Nick Zukauskas

critique.

Photos: Nick Zukauskas

"When a form of representation is new, it also gives us a way of envisioning a new kind of architecture."

—Andrew Zago

Photos: Nick Zukauskas

CLUB

in conversation.

ANDREW ZAGO.

Andrew Zago
with Jasmine Benyamin

Jasmine Benyamin

One of the topics you discussed at great length during your time with the students was architectural representation. More precisely you outlined an argument for the importance of urban representation and drawing's role therein. Can you expand on this?

Andrew Zago

Drawing with a capitol D is a very particular thing, and I have a certain responsibility to foster it at SCI-Arc, given the preponderance of large renderings. Notwithstanding, the technological considerations, these renderings still follow the tenets of Renaissance perspective. Why would you think that a perspective is a new idea in drawing? What a student may think is radical is actually a project that is deeply conservative and even retrogressive.

With classical Cartesian one-point perspectives, you have a case where its history was one of a form of representation that offered a thrilling set of new possibilities, but that is now a default for our understanding of how space is composed. It is best served to promote and isolate the object-ness of objects: in other words, when space is reduced it becomes a background, a negative featureless one against which objects can be prominently displayed. There is no confusion between an orthographically produced cube and the space it sits in, and in an unconsidered way, buildings do a very good job of behaving exactly like cubes. These objects have clear outlines and internal geometries that produce outwardly bounded corners.

They have a persistence in time, clear separation from the background, and a certain solidity. Simply by looking, we can easily understand its three dimensionality.

That working space that you assemble—that drawing, that model that particular projection system—inflects itself and permeates fairly deeply into what the project itself is. You have to examine the tools through which you are making something. Drawings are those things that architects produce when the project does not exist yet, and they don't know what it looks like.

JB

At one point in your conversations with students, you made a distinction between drawings and (mere) pictures. Can you elaborate?

AZ

In a way I was sort of making a distinction somewhat sarcastically between drawings and pictures. When you present a project and all you show me are pictures, then I ask: "Can you show me a drawing instead?" There's no such thing as an instantaneous picture. Every picture takes a certain amount of time. Historically, the lion's share of architectural history has been drawing. Today, its more complicated—and in fact, maybe (if we think of Gaudi's structural models) it has been more complicated for a while.

JB

Yes, drawings have occupied fluctuating roles in the discipline.

AZ

Whereas you could argue that drawings had a kind of autonomy, a certain "art-ness," over the latter half of the 20th century, we have witnessed what I would call the decay of drawing: in the post-war period—especially in the US—drawings became a means to indicate some future construction. I would call these kinds of drawings "pictures of buildings."

But then came along figures like John Hedjuk, and Bernard Tschumi, but especially the "micro mega" and "Chamber Works" suites of drawings by Daniel Libeskind when he was still at Cranbrook—they produced drawings that were independent problems in and of themselves.

Another example of an evolution of representation and of what that might mean would be the chair projects. We worked with a number of precedents including the Barcelona Chair, the Reitveld Chair, and Terragni's Casa del Fascio chair. We made a series of films with rotating chairs. Could we re-make the chairs while they rotated? What if you then cut sections through them as they moved? I would refer to this scenario as an effort to shift from conventional models of representation to degeneration.

JB

Thinking of Tschumi, movement in space is also central to your own re-conception of representation.

AZ

Yes. We can think of another analogy related to the distinguishing features between cubism and futurism—whereas in the former, several views of the same object are registered on the picture plane, in the latter, several points in time are used to capture the same object or event. Cameras can do the latter, but can we mobilize this concept toward new techniques of drawing?

JB

How do these thoughts extend to issues of representation more globally?

AZ

One of my interests has been to address broader questions: How do you draw a representation? How do you make a drawing of a perspective, rather than a perspective drawing? In reference to the Renaissance Urbino panels of Ideal cities and Piranesi's Carceri series, is the former merely documenting and the other projecting? Or do they both fall under this category?

A culture's ability to read forms of representation evolves and changes quite rapidly over time. When a form of representation is new it also gives you a way of envisioning a new kind of architecture, and in the case of this workshop, a new kind of urbanism.

JB

Switching to another topic, Godzilla was often invoked during the charrette—in particular his original avatar created by Ishiro Honda in 1954—and became a kind of mascot for the project brief. Why Godzilla?

AZ
This comes out of stories according to Jeff Kipnis. I haven't checked his footnotes, but he claims when the original *King Kong* was released, audiences ran out of the theater screaming because they were so frightened. Now, it's rather amusing to watch the original *King Kong*, but at the time it was actually shocking. In other words, the humor and awkwardness with which we might associate the original *Godzilla* might be really funny today, but in 1954, no one would know what you were talking about.

Some examples of architectural analogs would be Arato Isozaki's renderings of the Brooklyn Museum, which were then inserted into the background decor of a chiropractor's office in the first season of *Seinfeld*. Another example: The artist David Reid digitally inserting his work into the background of Alfred Hitchcock's *Vertigo*. In the context of the workshop, the scenario was: Make some dumb Photoshop things and drop them into images of Chicago, as if to say that it just showed up one day.

JB
Turning to the title of your school-wide lecture, "I Object." How did you come up with it?

AZ
These days I mostly work on the titles of things. This is an important aspect of projects. When I work with thesis students, one of the first questions is, "can we think of a good title for this thing?"

When I first got involved with architecture, there was a period where I objected to the whole idea of making buildings; that axiomatically one was outside architecture. Part of the implication here was that once you made a building, the propensity was for it to become an object, and that counter to the idea of the building was the literal metric sense of a form as an object. But there also exists another sense—a phenomenal one—of how things work in space. This mode of thinking creates a more nuanced condition. Can one look at the particular objecthood of things and see if one could displace or loosen them in order to promote a new kind of architectural condition? To this end, I started making a series of diagrams a couple of years ago. At one point, I pulled out my copy of Rudolf Arnheim's *Art and Visual Perception*, and I thought, "dammit this guy copied me exactly in 1955."

Kidding aside, this thinking is not without influence within the discourse of architecture. I have a growing interest in color in three dimensions. I think that Robert Slutzky also referred to him in *Transparency: Literal and Phenomenal*. As a fairly fundamental text at least for the students at SCI-Arc, it is interesting to note that Slutzky too emerged from Josef Albers's training. One of the takeaways from the reading—both in terms of drawing, but also in terms of color—is that two-dimensional images that tend also toward three-dimensional readings create spatial ambiguities that can offer powerful lessons. What is funny about their essay is that they then apply this logic to buildings, which are a priori three-dimensional.

Anyway, maybe the title shouldn't have been "I Object" but "stuff we do at Zago Architecture."

JB

These remarks seem to follow your earlier comments about perspective drawings.

AZ

Cartesian objects in perspectival space stand out like exclamation marks. For various reasons, I disagree (I object, if you will) with this reading. I believe there are powerful conditions and effects that can be generated by carefully analyzing and displacing a series of objects.

What I am interested instead is actually the object as asterisk. Using another analogy, when someone's world record time has an asterisk next to it, there is some ambiguity to it—maybe there was doping involved. Similarly, I am drawn more to objects that have ambiguous relationships vis a vis space—an attitude of inflection. In my early partnership with Bahram Shirdel and our practice AKS RUNO, we were working with these ideas that we referred to as a "disciplined relaxation" of geometry, which later Jeffrey Kipnis named "weak form." What does it mean? Can you ever make something that doesn't quite add up to geometry? Something that you can't quite get a complete picture of?

JB

How much of this thinking has been influenced by your background in fine arts?

AZ

When I went into architecture from the fine arts, I was at Harvard. This was a time when postmodernism was very much in its ascendancy, and frankly I didn't understand it at all.

My background was a bit different and I fundamentally didn't comprehend. Art school at Michigan didn't provide a particularly good education, but it coincided with a few important details: Very late in his career, the Austrian gestalt art theorist Rudolf Arnheim gave a lecture, and I was able to take a very large lecture class with him. Vince Castagnacci was also at the school, and he worked closely with Sewell Sillman who knew Albers at Yale and worked on the color sequences. Castagnacci was very much from this school of thought—a fairly straight line that emanated from the Bauhaus. The discourse they fostered underlined a certain attitude toward form and composition, geometry and space, which I in turn was imbued with. Suddenly people at the GSD start telling me, "No it's not about that, it's about what precedent you are making reference to." You were playing in a hall of mirrors essentially. I didn't understand it and nearly dropped out.

I must say that it was Harry Cobb (who was sheriff at the time, and who subsequently became a good friend) intervened that year when I almost dropped out. He later recalled to me that he woke up one night in the middle of the summer and said to himself, "What have I done?" and it was in that moment that he decided to bring in a whole new crew of people. Peter Eisenman was given a multi-year contract, and Jeff Kipnis and Daniel Libeskind were recruited.

I always thought it important to think about architecture as a work of art, and that it has a complex relationship to space—one that relates to form as I understand it. In contradiction to "shape," form implies a more complex relationship to space. In other words, if a shape begins to actually suggest that space that it exists in, then it becomes form.

2017

together.
whenever.

"His work was elegant and in good taste, and most importantly, his architecture was not unnecessarily demanding on the functional or intellectual levels. His architecture could be altered internally without vitiating the power of its external appearance."

—Stanley Tigerman
Mies Van Der Rohe: A Moral Modernist Model

Cover of *The Glass House: A Home for Gracious Living*, (1957) showing an interior view of a unit with Holabird and Root's Art Deco Palmolive Building (1929) in the background.

J. MAYER H.

The sharing economy increasingly becomes our new reality when family structures, nomadic lifestyles, and economic challenges demand new forms of how we live. The MASTERcrit workshop questions and rethinks innovative concepts of sharing for new housing project strategies.

Mine, yours, ours. We see further transformations of ownership, time-based usage, the common use of services provided and the organization of social activities, which transform our traditional understanding of housing and home. John Paul Ricco argues in his book that "the decision between us" is "shared separation." We will explore the balance between intimacy and privacy, between the individual and the communal, between mine, yours, and ours, between retreat and involvement or even between a personal touch and our shared tastes.

All programmatic elements of a housing project are on display for rethinking what is shared and what is separated: garden, roof, balconies, bathrooms, kitchens, mobility, pools, sleeping, etc. The logistics of sharing will need to take into consideration the presence of apps and social media.

We will start with a given building, the Mies van der Rohe Lake Shore Drive Apartments (860/880 Lakeshore Drive). The buildings will be "unmade" and "erased" in reference to John Paul Ricco's writing in order to then reassemble or "unbecome" a new architectural proposal for future housing. What needs to be defined are the components of an architectural program that are to be shared and the ones that remain separated. An analysis of apps that are part of this sharing economy will help us understand the logistics at hand.

This MASTERcrit charette proposes new relational organizations within the building and with its context.

—Jürgen Mayer H.

MASTERcrit*_2017
JUERGEN MAYER H.
UNIVERSITY of WISCONSIN - MILWAUKEE
SCHOOL OF ARCHITECTURE AND URBAN PLANNING
* [/ˈmɑːstəˌ/krid]
noun ; derived from master class [/ˈmɑːstəˌklɑːs/]
1. a class or session given to exceptional students of
a particular discipline by an expert of the discipline.

charette.

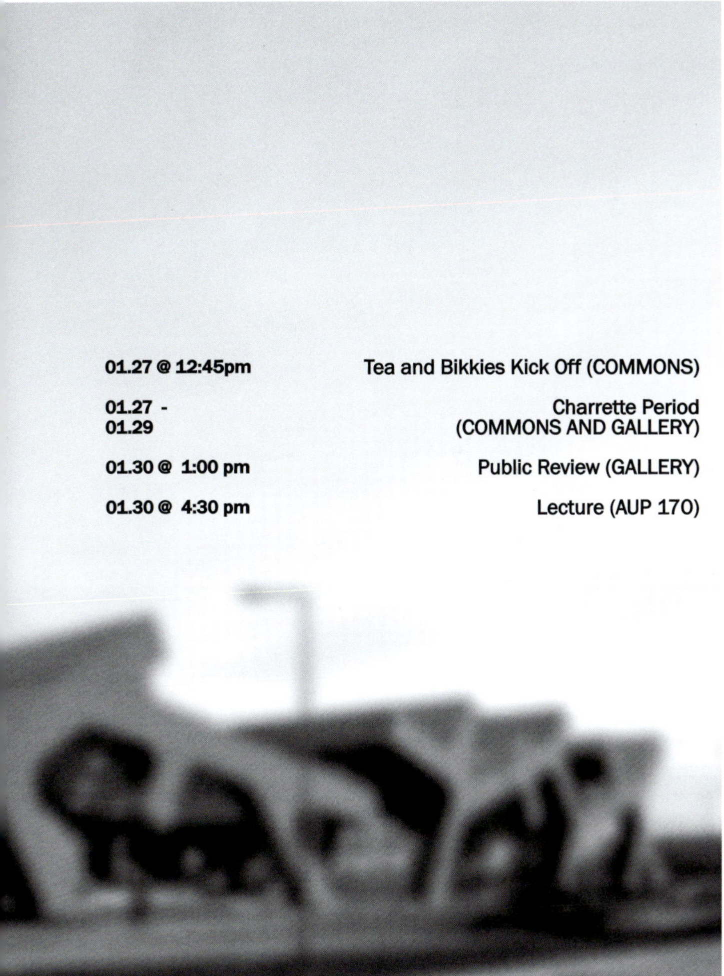

01.27 @ 12:45pm	Tea and Bikkies Kick Off (COMMONS)
01.27 - 01.29	Charrette Period (COMMONS AND GALLERY)
01.30 @ 1:00 pm	Public Review (GALLERY)
01.30 @ 4:30 pm	Lecture (AUP 170)

Do not
leave the
woodshop
with
safety
glasses.

"Strangely, and almost without precedent, American society came to look to architecture as a means of establishing cultural credibility."

—Stanley Tigerman

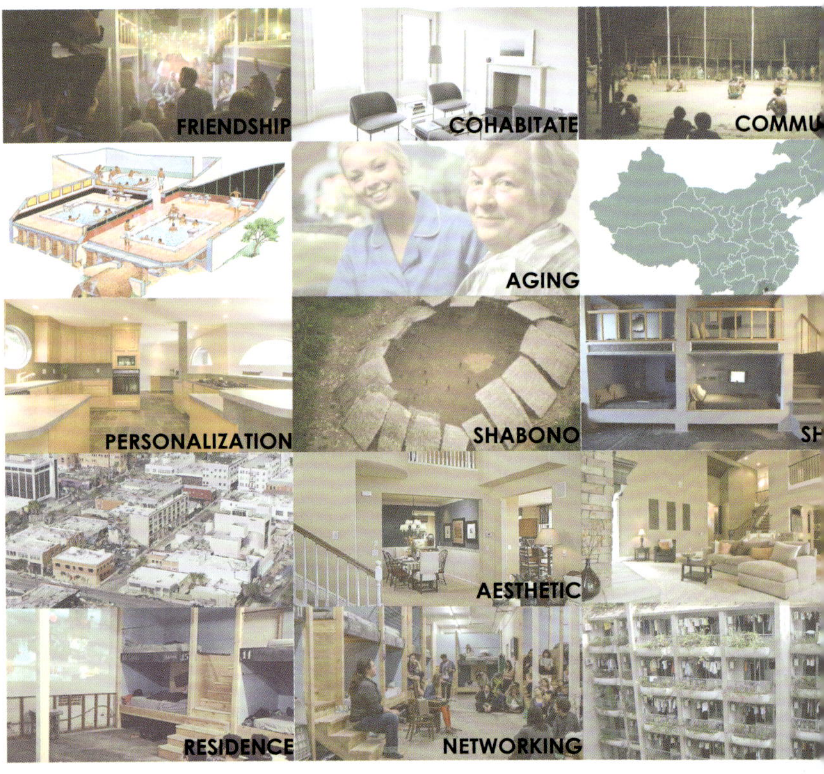
FRIENDSHIP
COHABITATE
COMMU
AGING
PERSONALIZATION
SHABONO
AESTHETIC
RESIDENCE
NETWORKING

research.

As an initial component of the charrette, the students embarked on individual research projects in order to generate a collective knowledge base for their design interventions. Social and collective aspects of living spaces were explored and presented to the group, to better understand the project as a whole.

How Beige Took Over American Homes

In the early 2000s the beige plague ran rampant through American homes. Everywhere you turned, a new wall was being painted "crème," a sofa was upholstered in an "oatmeal" fabric, and throw pillows were offered in "coffee" and "sand." Mortgage reforms allowed more people to purchase homes, and the booming home-improvement TV networks became a platform of (nearly free) design expertise. Design advice given to sell your home was now the advice people were using in order to decorate their homes. All sense of personalization was lost in order to make your home the most profitable—someone else had to be able to see themselves in it.

ROAM: INTERNATIONAL CO-LIVING SPACES

CURRENT LOCATIONS: LONDON, MIAMI, BALI, MADRID
COMING SOON: TOKYO AND SAN FRANCISCO

Roam is a new startup that wants your next office to be in a boutique hotel, anywhere in the world. Designed to meet the freedoms of the digital world, Roam offers co-living spaces in four locations for $500/week, where you are provided with a private bed and bath, and with shared kitchen/co-working spaces. The company hopes to draw young professionals looking to explore the world, but not have to give up their jobs, allowing them to work remotely with ultra hi-speed internet.

What Are The World's Loneliest Cities?

Where: Vancouver, Canada, and Shenzhen, China

In Shenzhen, migrant workers live where they work. The factory becomes the neighborhood. Housed in the dormitories, the migrant workers risk high rates of suicide. Contrary to Shenzhen, in Beijing the migrant workers bring village values to the large city. In Vancouver, loneliness is considered a public health threat. High housing costs cause renters to become unhappy and see other people leading richer lives with cheaper rents. The higher number of renters translates to transience and lower community engagement. Older people are among the loneliest demographic with smaller households. While older people tend to be lonely, they also tend to seek more privacy and do not need a lot of social interaction. The quality of social interaction and a balance between the city and privacy fights loneliness. Humans can be inherently territorial but need social interaction nonetheless. Thankfully, loneliness passes.

Below: Section modules

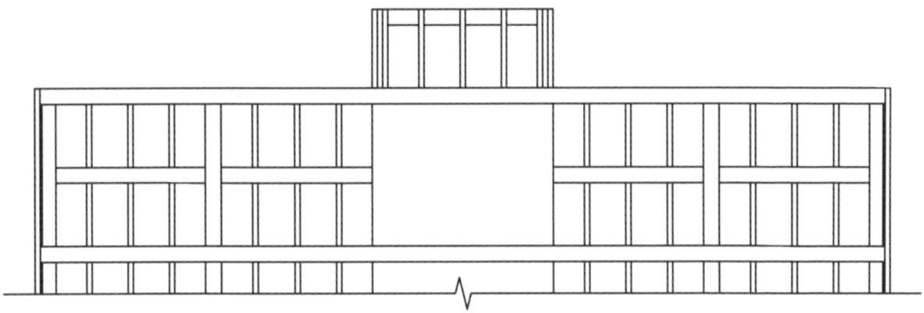

The Original Sharing Economy

There is no such thing as private property. The original sharing economy consisted of sharing property, allowing for a nomadic way of life. Hunting and gathering offered a way to survive with a bound of plentiful goods. The transition from a sharing economy coincided with the introduction of farming. With farming, individuals could store produce and could relish on the fruits of their labor. This individualism still existed with a communal location until the early 1700s. These common areas that preceded normal farming conventions led to sharing tools by farming in long rows rather than square-shaped parcels. Once the transition occurred from communal land use to large landowner-controlled parcels, the mindset of the society changed. Now people were not invested in the land and saw labor as just fulfilling a land-use agreement not to obtain resources. Today, ownership remains private with technology being the largest shared resource.

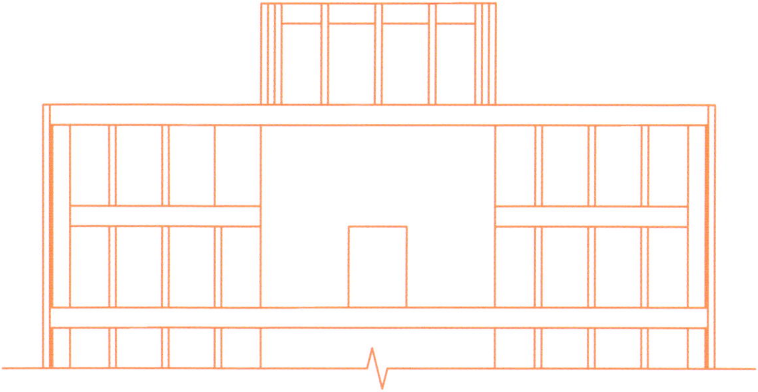

house rules.

The original House Rules are, unsurprisingly, very much a product of their time. The 22 points outlined reflect a culture of politeness and propriety that defined the exceptionalism of post-war America. They constitute nothing less than an official Code of Conduct. Students used this document as a concrete point of departure to pursue new programmatic interventions. As a result, they effectively dismantled the old class of tenants and ushered a new progressive community of co-inhabitants.

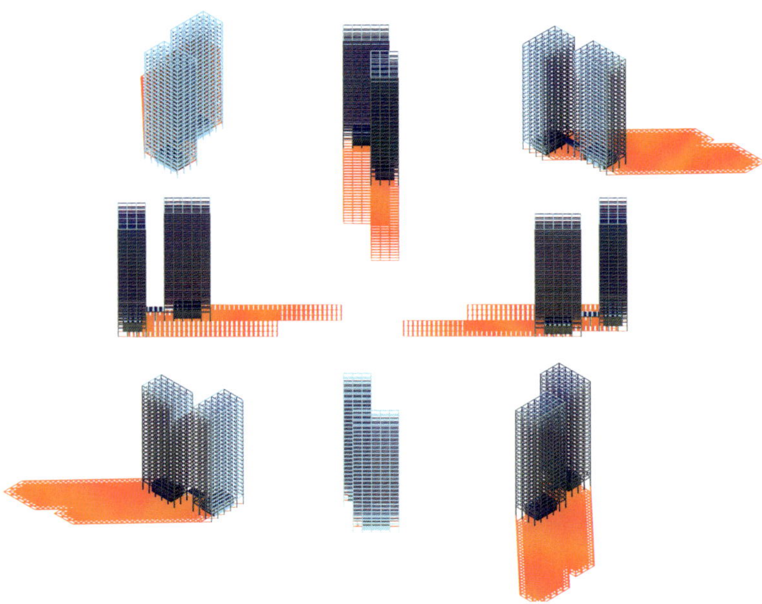

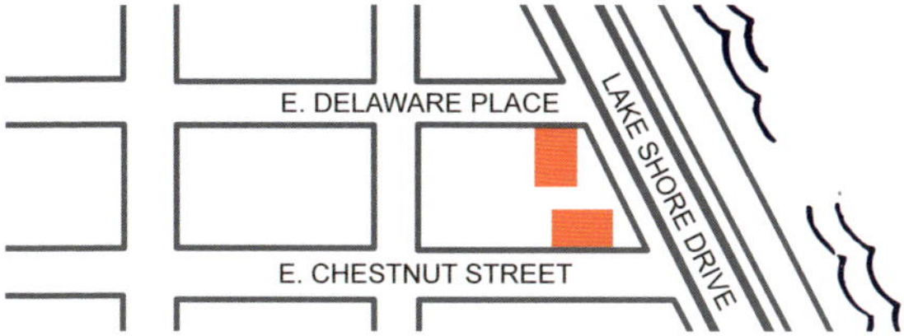

"In a setting of simple majestic beauty, the spectacular twin towers of glass and steel at 860–880 Lake Shore Drive—now known familiarly as the Glass House—brought to Chicago and to the world a new concept in apartment design.

Boldly rectangular, unembellished, their framework of steel and aluminum sheathed in sheets of glass, the 26-story buildings house 271 apartments—three and six rooms—skillfully planned for grcious and comfortable cooperative living.

Designed by Ludwig Mies van der Rohe, world-renowned archtect, the buildings express a mid-twentieth-century concept of design of our technological age and stand today as a distinguished contribution to modern architecture—the first multiple-apartment glass house.

The 860–880 buildings are now fully occupied by a carefully selected group of tenant-owners. Business executives, attorneys, architects, physicians, and members of many other distinguished professions enjoy the privileges of Glass House living.

"CHICAGO'S FINEST LOCATION"

In all of Chicago there is not a more desirable location for gracious modern living than the Glass House. This historic "first" is further dramatized by its unique lakeside setting.

With housing shortages in the area and lake frontage no longer available, tenant-ownership in the Glass House assumes new import. Both buildings and the land on which they are located have increased in value from their original cost of $5,850,871.00.

While nearby, newly constructed apartments lease for exceedingly high prices, tenant-owners of Glass House apartments, under the protection of coo perative ownership, continue to enjoy comparatively reasonable assessment rentals, the ever-increasing value of their equities, and the welcome benefits of interest and real estate tax deductions."

Excerpt from *The Glass House: A Home For Gracious Living* (1957) 860–880 Tenant Owners Association

HOUSE RULES

860-880 LAKE SHORE DRIVE

CHICAGO 11

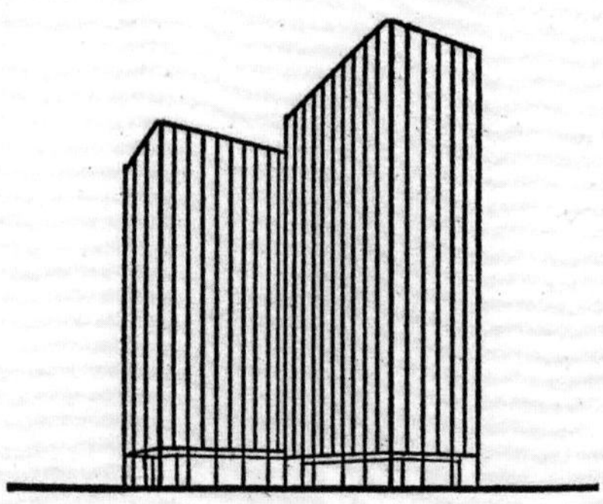

TENANT OWNERS COMMITTEE

1957

HOUSE RULES

1. The public halls, sidewalks and stairways shall not be obstructed or used for any other purposes than for ingress to and egress from the apartments.

2. No baby carriages, velocipedes, or bicycles will be allowed in the halls, passageways, areas or courts of the buildings.

3. Children shall not be permitted to loiter or play on the stairways or in the halls or lobby.

4. Halls and stairways shall not be used for the storage of furniture or other articles.

5. No automobiles shall be parked within fifteen feet of either side of the sidewalk canopy nor shall doormen or other building employees not specifically charged with such duties be requested or permitted to park cars for tenants.

6. Servants and employees of tenants and persons making deliveries to tenants shall not use the passenger elevators except when accompanied by their employers.

7. All provisions, milk, ice, groceries, furniture, bicycles, boxes and the like merchandise shall be taken into or removed from the demised premises through the rear door of said buildings only. All damages to the buildings, caused by the moving or carrying of articles therein, shall be paid by the tenant, or person in charge of such articles.

8. Tenants attired in beach or bathing wear shall be required to use the service elevator and entrance.

9. Tenants will not be allowed to put their names in any entry, passageway, vestibule, hall or stairway of the building, except in the proper places provided therefor in connection with their use of the apartments occupied by them.

10. No sign, signal, advertisements, or illumination shall be inscribed or exposed on or at any window or other part of the apartment buildings, except such as shall be approved by Lessor.

11. No radio or television aerial or connection shall be installed by the tenants outside of their respective apartments without the consent of Lessor.

12. No tenant shall make or permit any disturbing noises in the buildings by himself, his family, friends or servants; nor do or permit anything to be done by such persons that will interfere with the rights, comforts or convenience of other tenants. No tenant shall play or suffer to be played any radio,

television or musical instrument in the demised premises between the hours of 11 o'clock P.M. and the following 8 o'clock A.M., if the same shall disturb or annoy any other occupant of the building.

13. Animals and birds are not allowed in the demised premises, except by special permission of Lessor.

14. In order to assure a uniform outside appearance to the buildings, it is expected that Lessor will furnish outside drape linings. Such linings, if furnished by Lessor, shall be used by tenants and no other drapes, drape linings, or other window hangings of any sort shall be hung between the windows and the drape linings furnished by Lessor, and no shades, awnings or window guards may be used by tenants without the approval in writing of Lessor.

15. No tenants shall interfere in any manner with any portion either of the heating or lighting apparatus in or about the demised premises nor in or about the building containing the same.

16. The water closets and other water apparatus shall not be used for any purpose other than that for which they were constructed, and no sweepings, rubbish, rags, paper, ashes or other substances shall be thrown therein. Any damage resulting to them from misuse of any nature or character whatever shall be paid by the tenant who shall cause it.

17. Wet garbage shall be wrapped in paper and deposited in receptacles provided for that purpose.

18. Nothing shall be thrown or emptied by the tenants or their servants out of the windows or doors, or down the passages, courts, or in the building areas, nor shall anything be hung from the outside of the windows or placed on the outside window sills.

19. The water shall not be left running any unreasonable or unnecessary length of time in the demised premises.

20. No rugs shall be beaten in the halls, nor dust, rubbish or litter swept from the demised premises or any room thereof into any of the halls or entryways of the building containing said premises, except under the direction of the janitor.

21. Laundry work shall be done only in the place or places set aside by Lessor for this purpose in the building of which the demised premises are a part, and only the equipment provided by Lessor for this purpose shall be used.

22. Lessor reserves the right to amend these rules and to make such other rules and regulations from time to time as may be deemed needful for the safety, care and cleanliness of the premises and for securing the comfort and convenience of all of the occupants thereof.

HOUSE RULES

860-880 LAKE SHORE DRIVE

CHICAGO II

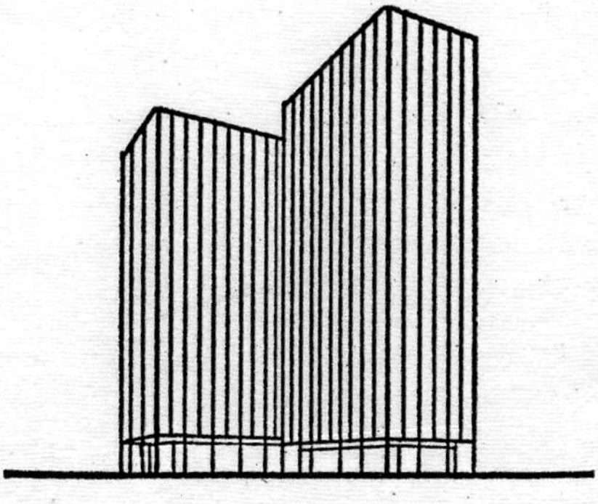

TOGETHER WHENEVER

2017

research.

HOUSE RULES

1.Public halls, sidewalks and stairways are encouraged to be used as social spaces.

2.Baby carriages, velocipedes, and bicycles will be allowed in the halls, passageways, areas or courts of the buildings as long as they do not obstruct the flow.

3.Children are encouraged to visit everyone in the building.

4.It is encouraged to leave furniture and other articles in the halls for all tenants to use as they please.

5.Floors 22-26 must abide by the 50:50 ratio.

6.In order to assure a uniform appearance to the pantry, all provisions, milk, ice, groceries, and the like merchandise shall be taken into the collective pantry, removed from the original packaging and stored in provided glass containers.

7.Both tenants and guest are permitted to wear casual attire on the 860-880 Lake Shore Drive premises.

8.Anyone who uses the fitness facility must learn about one tool in the collective workshop.

9.All tenants must use the fitness facility at least once a week.

10.Animals and birds are allowed in the demised premises.

11.The water closets and water apparatus shall be used for any purpose tenants' choose, so long as they don't partake in any morally questionable activities or cause damage to the facilities.

HOUSE RULES

12. Always flush. Toilet seats shall be left closed when not in use to control potential foul smells.

13. Clothes shall not be left in washer or dryer from an extended period of time past the end of each cycle. If done so, game points shall be void. If not involved in games, negative points shall be assigned.

14. No grown food shall be taken without appropriate arrangements.

15. Grower of plant, owns the plant.

16. All "wet garbage" – water – shall be disposed of in a communal receptacle and will be used to rehydrate the grounds.

17. Each unit is required to plant in its assigned planter in the rooftop garden.

18. Laundry cycles shall be timely managed by the users. If users are found engaged with games negligent of laundry cycle, negative rewards points shall be added to their account.

19. Place any and all literature into communal shelving.

20. Inform neighbors through BiblioTech when borrowing resources.

21. All explicit material shall be placed on the proper shelf.

22. Any rule can be modified if all tenants reach a consensus.

student work.

Bridgette	BINCZAK	M.Arch	2017
Kayla	DEVARES	BSAS	2017
Jack	GROVER	M.Arch	2019
Jackson	LEVERENZ	BSAS	2017
Tia	MILKOVA	M.Arch	2019
Jordan	NELSON	M.Arch	2017
Adam	OKNIN	BSAS	2017
Hrishkesh	PANDIT	M.Arch	2017
Sarah	TRAVER	M.Arch	2017
MARY	VANDERSTEEG	BSAS	2017

fun cycle.

J. MAYER H.

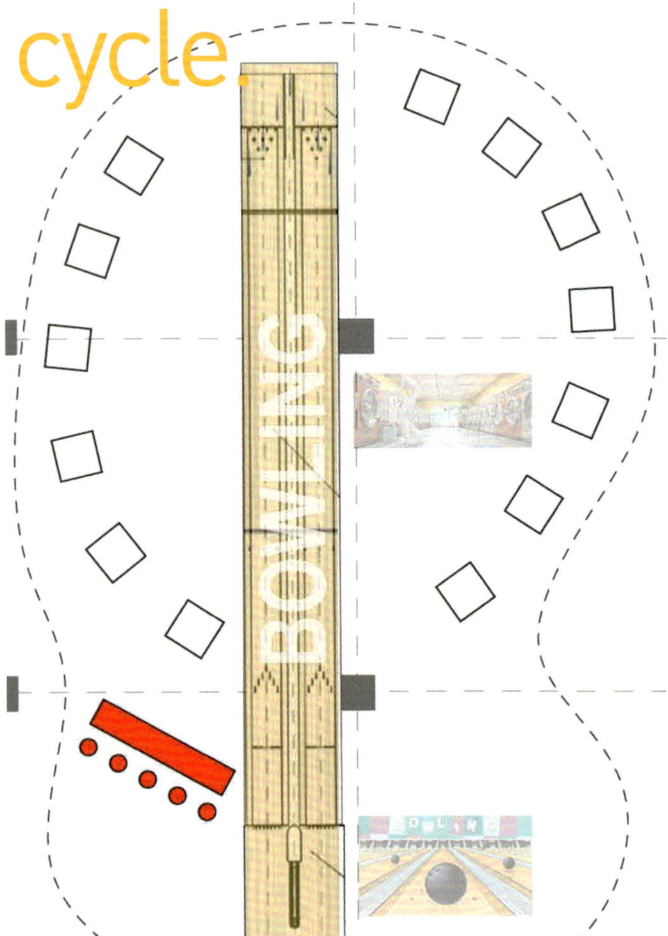

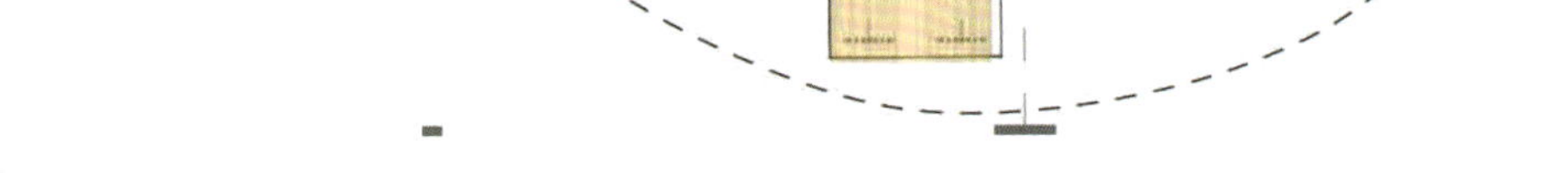

hrishikesh pandit.

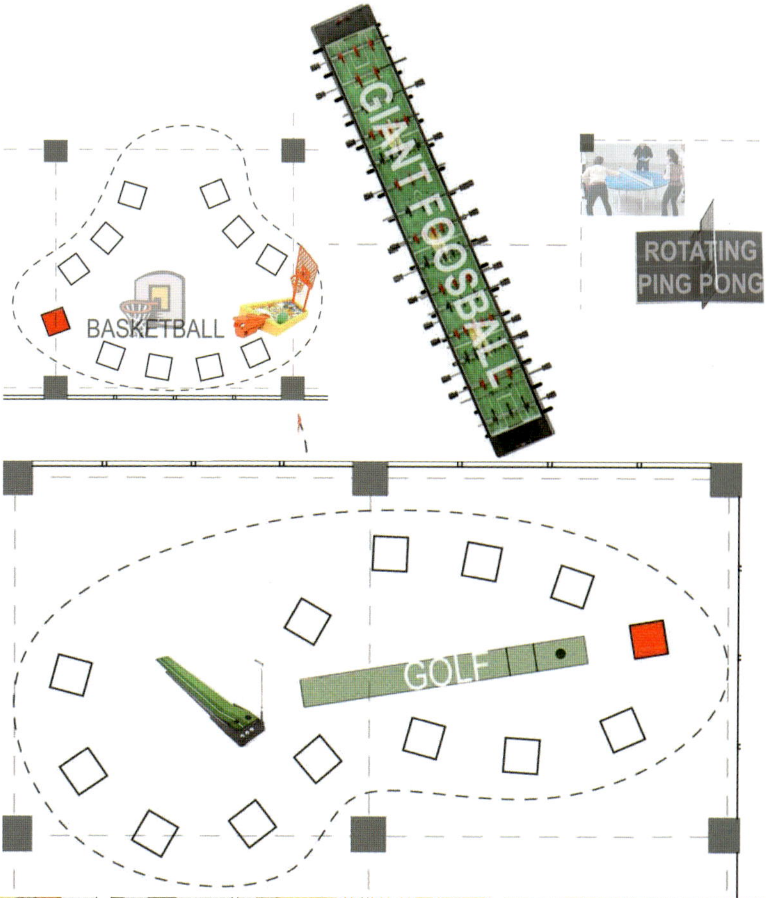

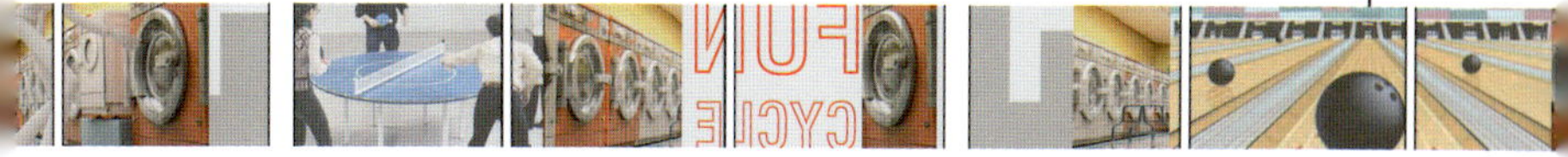

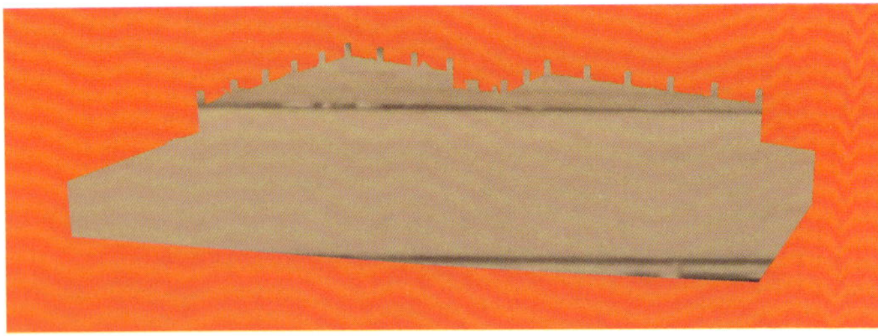

Pneumatic Modules

These modules would be designed to exist in two states: open (couch) or closed (bed). An open module can allow a guest to sit and work while remaining connected and social with nearby guests. The spaces could then be closed providing a "tube," which is private for sleeping, or removing oneself from the activity happening around them. These modules would be relatively lightweight, allowing them to bet set up virtually anywhere within the space.

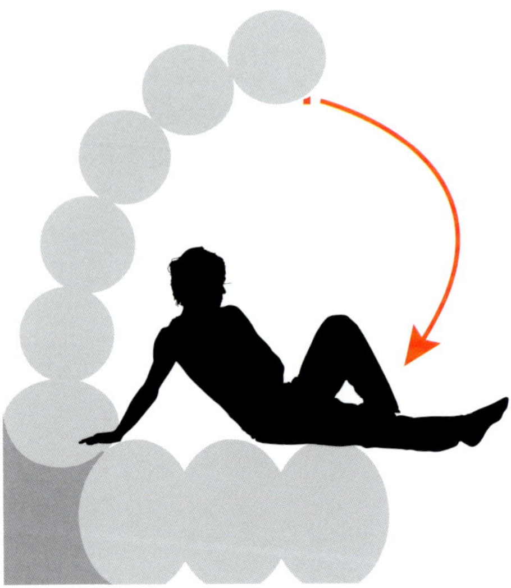

jack glover.

50: Fifty

This app is about connecting guests with each other, allowing them to communicate openly on a social media platform. The app allows users to reserve offices, request inflatables, find food nearby, and access the space all from one's mobile device. The app is meant to be the go-to support for all guests providing them the tools to live comfortably and to not only have a productive, but also a fun stay.

50 FIFTY

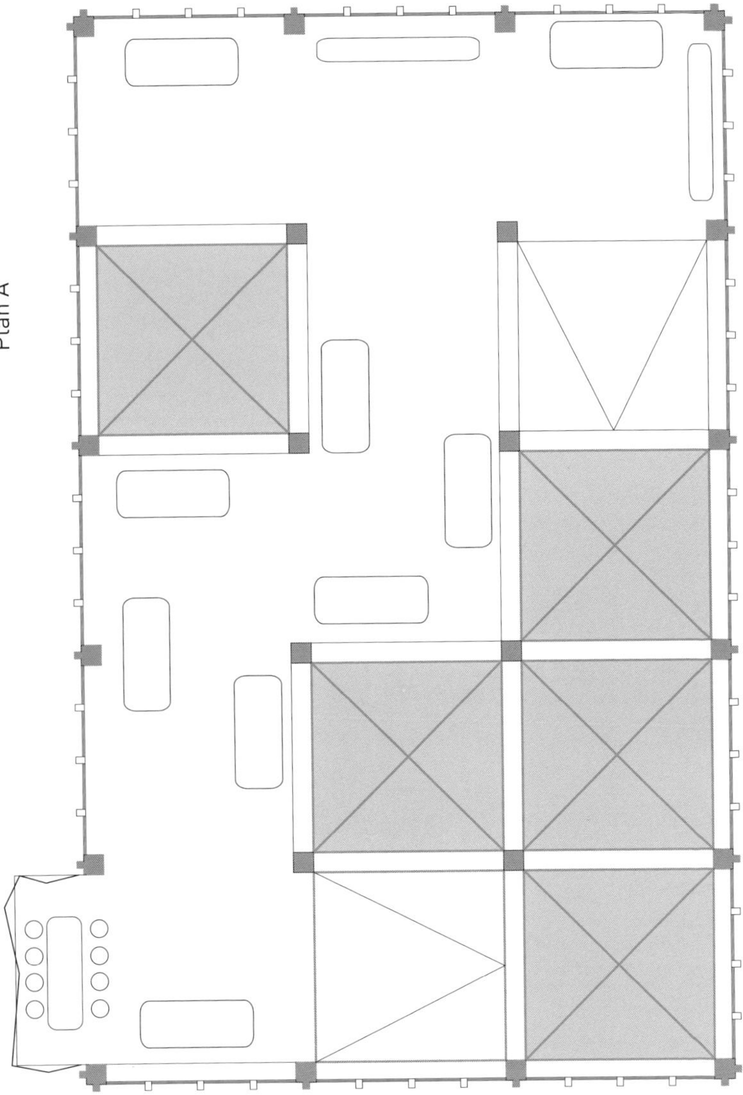

Plan A

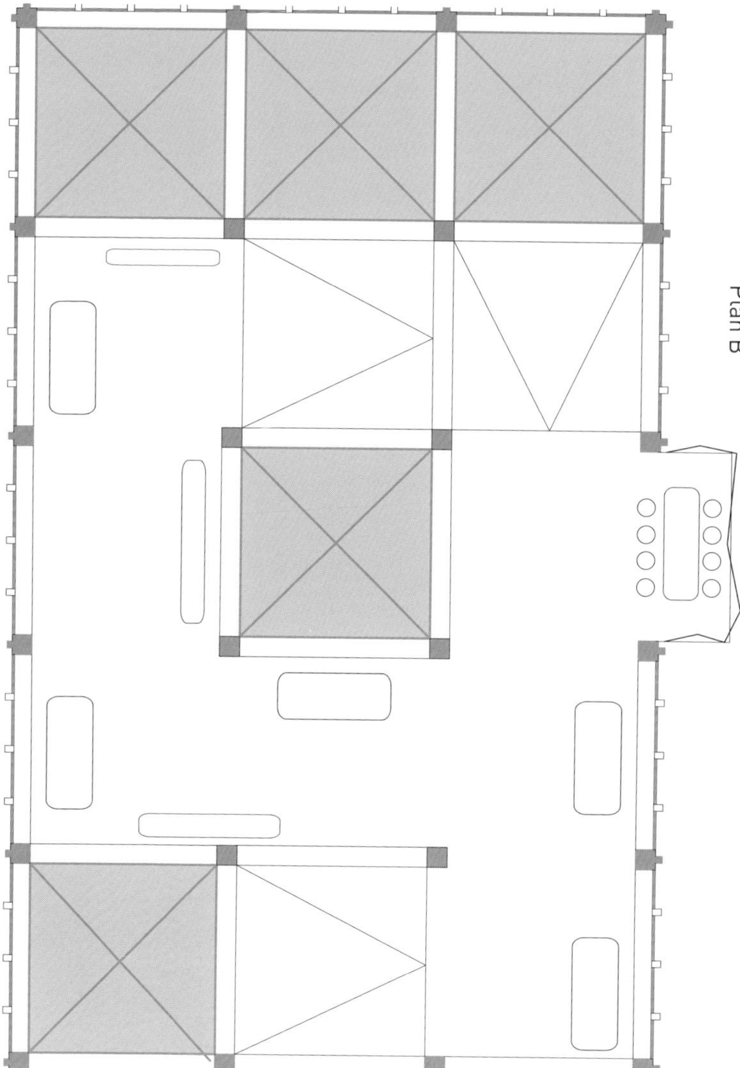

Plan B

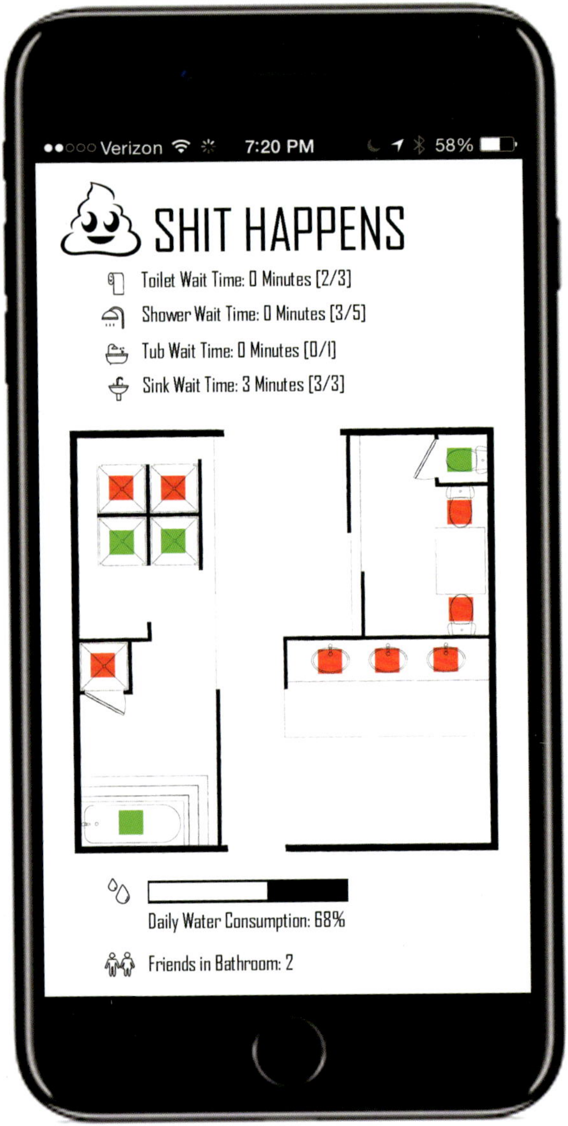
Verizon 7:20 PM 58%
SHIT HAPPENS
Toilet Wait Time: 0 Minutes [2/3]
Shower Wait Time: 0 Minutes [3/5]
Tub Wait Time: 0 Minutes [0/1]
Sink Wait Time: 3 Minutes [3/3]
Daily Water Consumption: 68%
Friends in Bathroom: 2

kayla de vares.

student work.

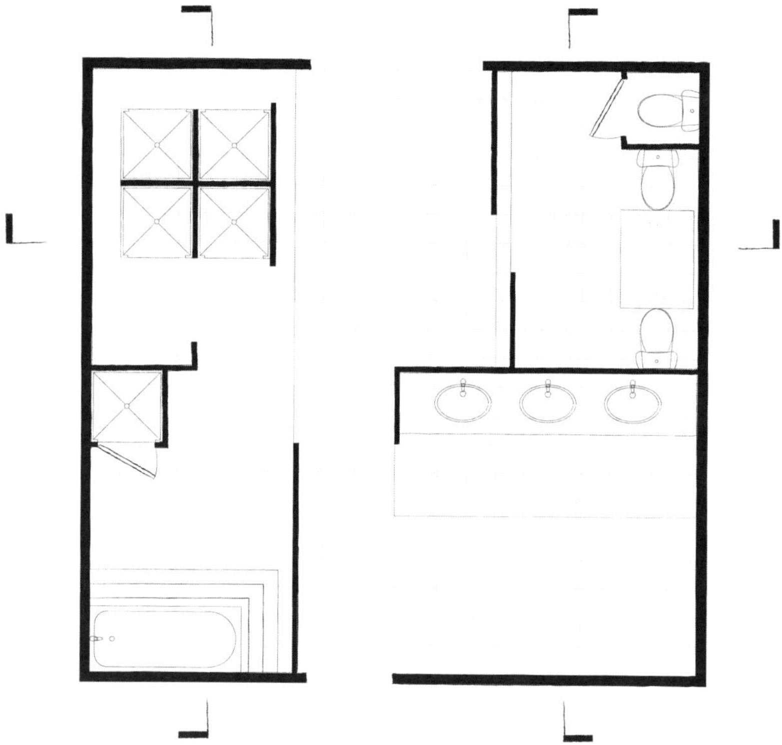

Plan

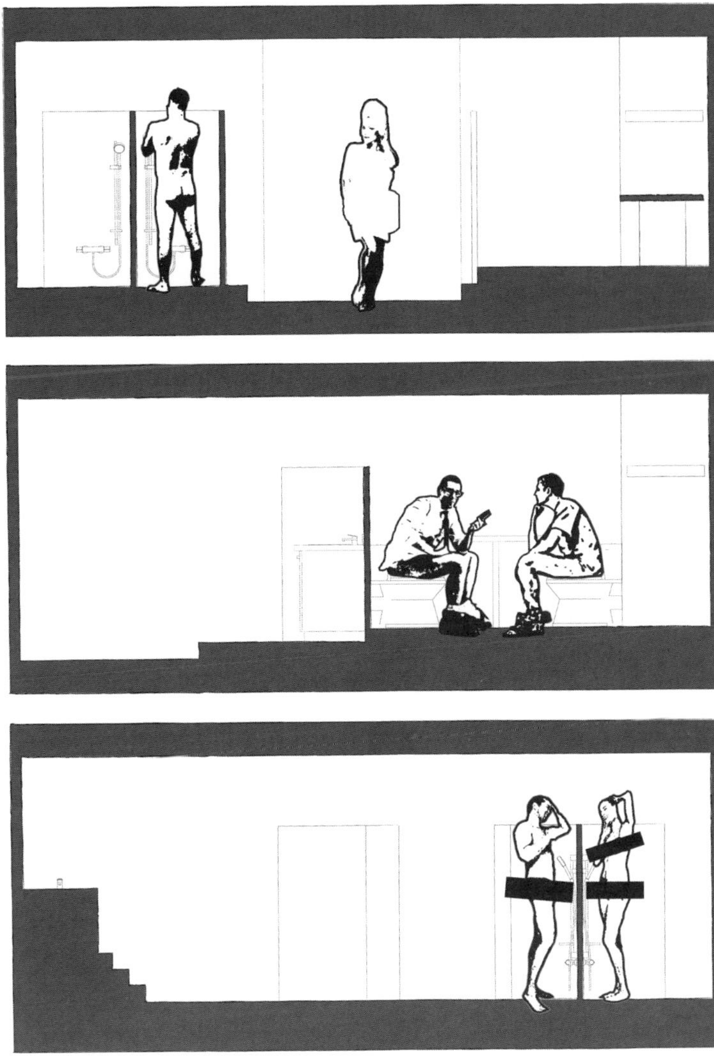

Section

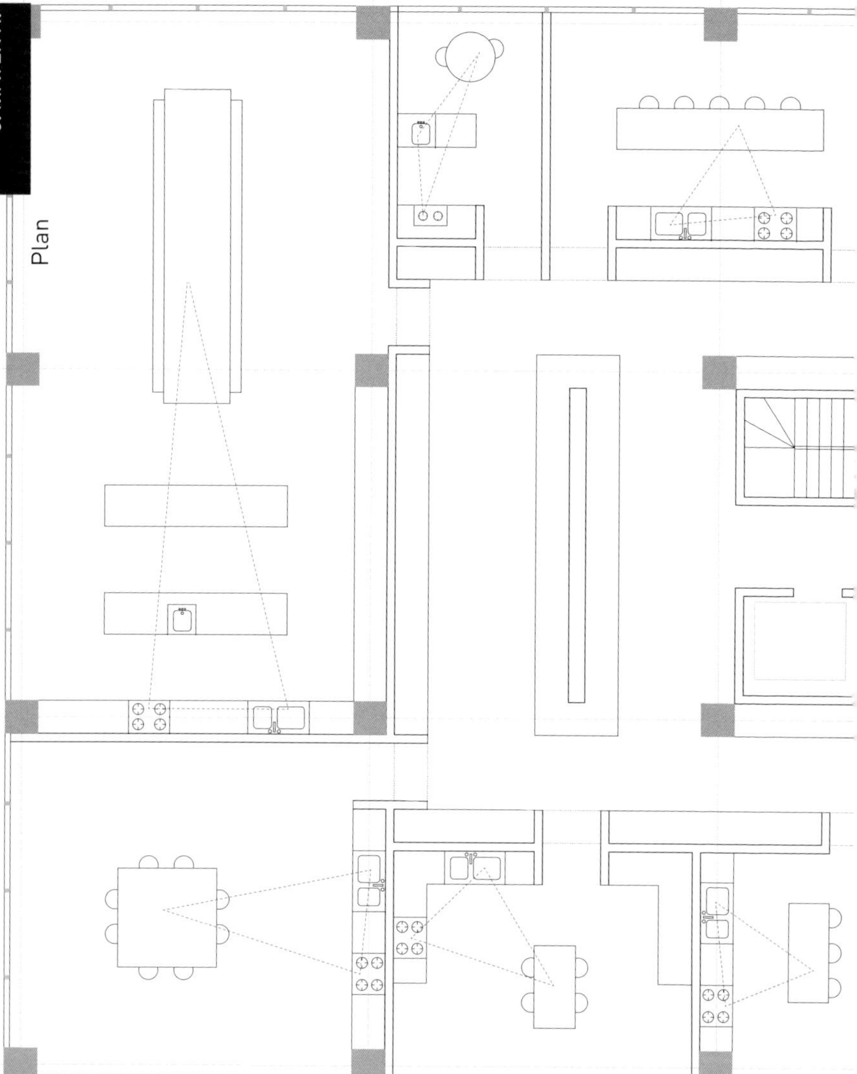

Plan

sarah traver.

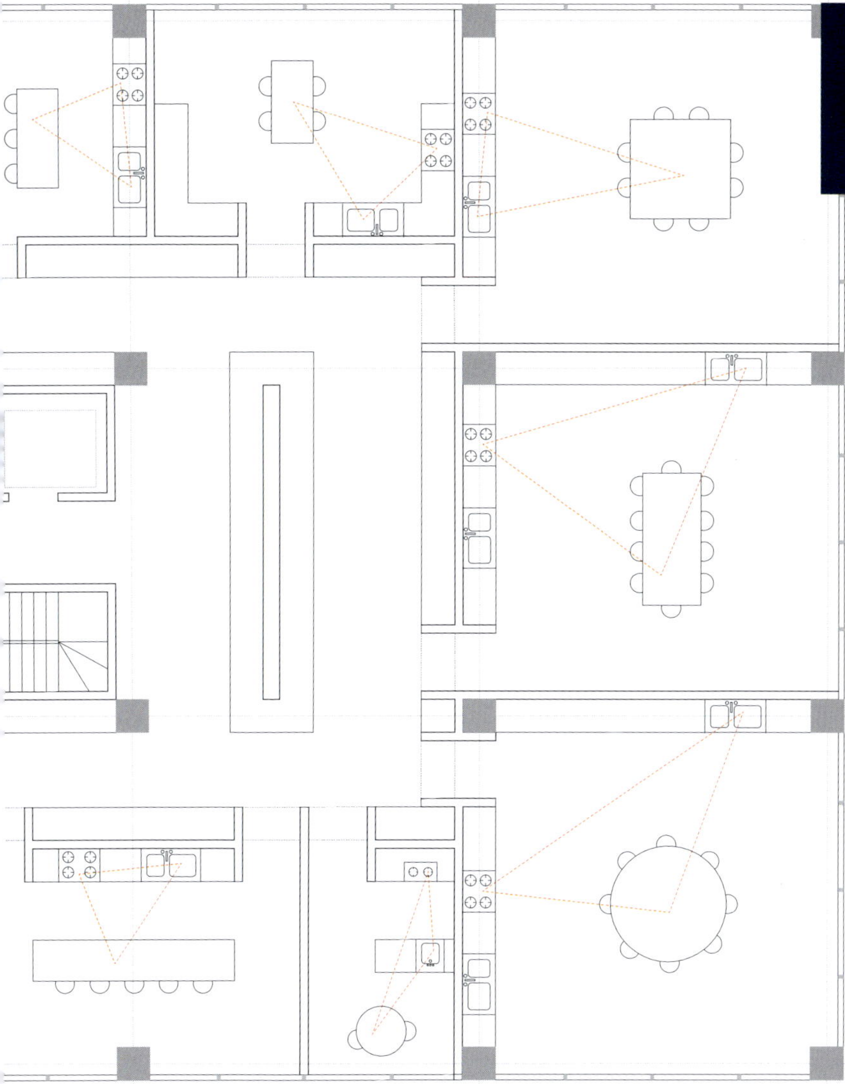

Plan Module

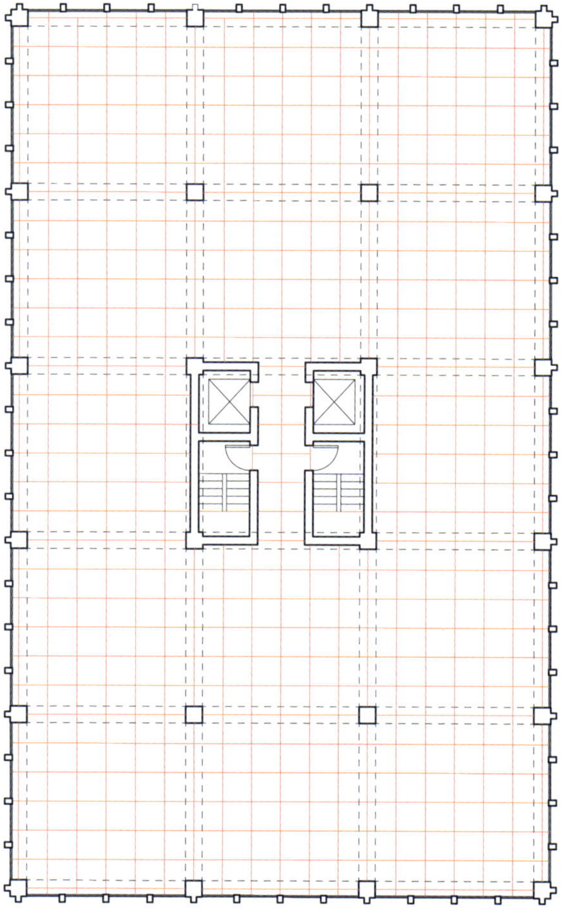

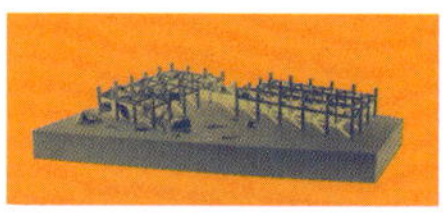

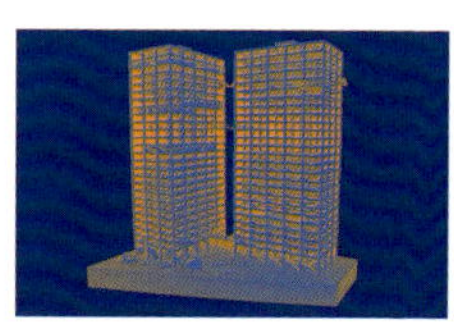

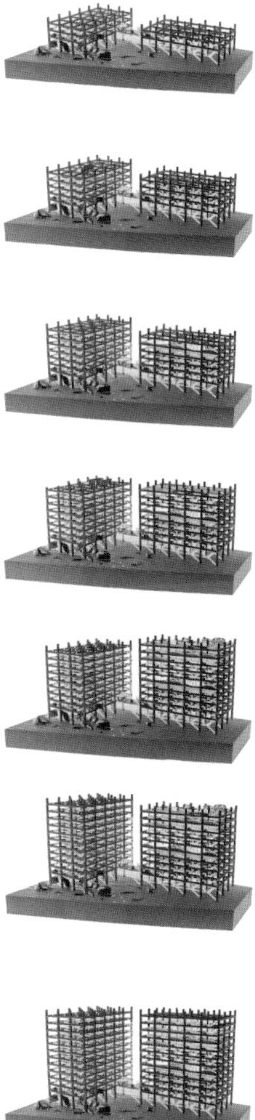

Photo: Eli Liebenow

critique.

Images from final critique
Photos: Eli Liebenow

Photos: Eli Liebenow

"Do the activities of the occupants drive the architecture, or does the architecture usher new activities?"

—Jürgen Mayer H.

in conversation.

J. MAYER H.

Photo: Joseph Wolfgang Ohlert

Jürgen Mayer H.

Jürgen Mayer H.
with Jasmine Benyamin

Jasmine Benyamin
In preparation for the charrette, and in our conversations about topics concerning HOUSE/HOUSING that interested you, we came up with the idea of: "TOGETHER.WHENEVER." If we de-couple this and go back to together and whenever, is it possible for you to sum up why these terms were relevant for you?

Jürgen Mayer H.
I thought it was important for the project brief to reflect what developments are taking place in modern society. What are the elements that bind families? What are the ways in which we identify and define families and their structures? I would argue that our friendships and the connections we foster are as important—if not more—than our familial ones.

If we extend the concept of "together" to include the ways in which we define sharing, more thoughts come to mind. "Sharing" has a positive ring to it. It gives us comfort and the freedom to care about what is important to us. The sharing economy is about trust—among individuals but also among communities. When we share, we take responsibility for each other. But be aware, not all sharing is about caring.

"Whenever" refers to the freedom of choice that each citizen has to opt out of collectivity. There must be space made for individual expression and intimacy among other factors. How can architecture celebrate community, but also allow for the fluidity of individual choice?

JB
What is it about the Lakeshore Drive Apartments that make them an appropriate site for asking some of these questions?

JMH
The fact that there are two of them, for one, and two is the smallest number to talk about when we refer to togetherness. They are individual objects that nonetheless share a common public space at the street level. What would happen if we reconfigured the floor plans and sections to reinforce sharing?

When Mies conceived the layouts of apartments, he was already rethinking conventions of domesticity. That was the 1950s. What if we were to revisit the plans and sections today? What alterations would we make? In addition to rethinking individual apartment configurations, students were also free to break through floor plates and double up volumes. They were also encouraged to think about the ways in which the two towers could be connected via bridges at upper stories. With these basic formal moves—and without upsetting the iconic steel frames—you create opportunities for new hybrid living and working spaces. The consolidation of services, of wet and dry, of stacked kitchens...these are all scenarios that reflect the particularly charged moment we find ourselves in today.

I also chose the site because of its proximity to Milwaukee. It is an icon that is firmly rooted in the history of modernism, but it was also a building that wasn't accessible only through photographs. The fact that the students could visit and document it in their own way was important. It is part of the canon but also part of their reality.

JB
What was the significance of having the students re-build the iconic framework of the towers as a point of departure?

JMH
Building a large model was important because it gave students the opportunity to physically engage with the structure. The frames literally became the frameworks for intervention. The profiles are still iconic and recognizable. Now emptied, students could re-think who the new target audiences for this pair of buildings could be.

Such a site has a high cultural and economic value, but if you were to re-envisage aspects of zoning and regulation of vis-à-vis the living spaces, you could likewise attract new constituencies. For example, could the buildings be reconfigured to accommodate multi-generational communities? Questions around ownership and flexibility were central to the discussion.

Despite the project's iconicity, the tactical decision to remove walls and floors and keep the grid of the structure gave us a kind of conceptual and organizational framework. It was recognizable yet voided enough that the students wouldn't feel constrained by preconceptions. They extracted the essence of the structure and built it large enough to imagine occupation.

JB

The theme "House/Housing" was one that was given to you, but not much else was provided in terms of a brief. You have touched a little bit already on how the concept of sharing could manifest in a structure such as the Lake Shore Drive Apartments. But the issue of scale also factors into the conversation: referring to a couple sharing a space implicates a different set of decisions than say sharing at a whole community scale.

JMH

I suppose the question of scale begs the question: How does one engage with their immediate environment? We might as a society be ready to re-negotiate how we want to live. Notions of so-called "private" space can be addressed within a larger space of sharing. Small clusters of say 10–12 people can cater to students and professionals alike. In fact, cities all over the world are addressing both demographics in this light.

There are essential spaces and non-essential spaces. There are temporary sharing scenarios (parties for example), and other areas like sleeping spaces can take up a smaller footprint. Living and working can take up a greater share. Perhaps in mixing these two groups, new social networks are fostered.

If you think about sharing in architectural terms—say modular dwelling units adjacent to more flexible/temporary programming—we can expand this model to the scale of the city. How do private and public operate at this other scale? How can cities address personal needs of individuals simultaneously with the needs of communities? How does this work? Well, in reality sometimes it does work and sometimes it doesn't. It is a matter of how expansively we are in our thinking about civic balance. There can be give and takes that can actually be fruitful for everyone involved. Spaces that engage in a kind of back and forth between giving and taking can constitute a joyful part of your life. Compromise can be joyful.

JB
What is architecture's role in managing or negotiating compromise at multiple registers?

JMH
As a starting point, we selected a few elements that had the potential to accommodate new interventions in a multiplicity of scenarios. One of them was the facade. Facades designate a division between outside and inside, they negotiate weather conditions, they communicate with neighbors. As thermal barriers, they provide climatic comfort. Another site of intervention could be the plaza at the ground floor. How do the buildings confront the city at the ground? How can the surrounding neighborhood be embraced and invited to participate in these new scenarios?

There are interior architectural elements like kitchens and terraces that can also easily be translated into communal scenarios. Others like toilets are less obvious, but that's where a lot of communication happens as we all know. Communality and singularity in this context also extend to unexpected parts of the program, and yet after all that is said and done, there are still expectations of privacy. I wasn't just interested in students creating "territories" that could be easily monitored and controlled. We were interested in creating a richness in freedom of choice by exploring the commons and offering a safe place for privacy.

JB
It is in these extremes of intimacy and retreat that we exist. The acknowledgment that we need both is what makes us co-exist.

JMH
Yes, and in this regard, the John Paul Ricco reading that was assigned to the students was important. He does not formulate

notions of separation and sharing in an explicit architectural context. But his perspectives on space and performance can be particularly informative in this scenario.

JB

If the premise of MASTERcrit is that we invite people to engage their own work in an academic setting, how does the work you engaged the students in relate to your own practice?

JMH

The topics I engaged the students in reflects my own interest in finding the potential in buildings to go beyond programmatic needs, and to find possible future spatial scenarios that are open to interpretation and appropriation. Ultimately, I am interested in action beyond potential.

I am very interested in social media in relation to placemaking, gathering, and connectivity. The evolution of platforms such as Facebook and Instagram should be reflected in what we do as architects. All of the students were asked to conceive of an app related to their proposal. Other questions I asked of the students, I too ask of myself. How can we find innovative ways to communicate ideas about buildings and cities? How has our use of digital social platforms changed how we attend to our everyday lives? How has the evolution of digital technology within our practice altered how we view architectural labor? How has it affected the way we design and build?

JB

What were your thoughts on MASTERcrit as a concept and alternative pedagogical model?

JMH

Pushing the students to address their individual agendas within the tight time frame of four days kept them out of their comfort zones. This is important because I think this pressure can also be motivating. Such a compressed space for making and problem solving allows for surprising outcomes.

Photo: Sarah Traver

MASTERcrit would not have been possible without the help and institutional support of all the faculty and staff at the University of Wisconsin-Milwaukee School of Architecture and Urban Planning. In particular: the David and Julia Uihlein Charitable Foundation and the following:

Chris Cornelius
Lisa Di Salvo
Bob Greenstreet
William Kruger
Ash Lettow
Sue McDonald
Kurt Meingast
Sharadha Natraj
Dolores Nordgren
Kyle Reynolds
Joan Simuncak
Tammy Taylor
Filip Tejchman
Karl Wallick
Mo Zell

Amin Mojtahedi assisted with the logistics and rollout of MASTERcrit 2015. Likewise, Whitney Moon was an invaluable collaborator for MASTERcrit 2016.

I am also indebted to my editors at ORO Editions, to Jake Anderson and Gordon Goff for their feedback, patience, and enthusiasm for the project.

acknowledgments.

Nick Zukauskas was part of the student cohort for the inaugural MASTERcrit. Since graduation, he continued his involvement with the project as graphic designer. Jake Anderson picked up the graphic mantle in the 11th hour to get the book ready for print.

Finally, this book is dedicated to the students and MASTERcritics.

Thank you.